Pocket Handbook

- FLIGHT CALCULATIONS
- WEATHER DECODER
- AVIATION ACRONYMS
- CHARTS AND CHECKLISTS
- PILOT MEMORY AIDS

FLIGHT TIME PUBLISHING
www.flight-time.com
1-877-926-6570
BY ART PARMA CFII, ATP, A&P/IA

PILOT'S POCKET HANDBOOK
Copyright © 2005 by Flight Time Publishing
Revised 2005, Fourth Edition
By Art Parma CFII, ATP, A&P/IA
ISBN 0-9631973-8-X
FTP-PPH-4

All rights reserved.

All rights reserved. No part of this book may be reproduced, stored in a retrieval system, or transmitted in any form or by any means, electronic, mechanical, photocopying, recording, or otherwise, without prior written permission from the publisher.

This book is for informational purposes only and is not intended to substitute any approved aircraft flight manual or official government publication.

TABLE OF CONTENTS

NAVIGATION AND PERFORMANCE 1
Navigation Formulas, Pilotage/Dead Reckoning, Rule of
Sixty, Crosswind Component Chart, Pressure Altitude,
Density Altitude Chart
WEIGHT AND BALANCE, ... 7
Weight Shift, MAC, Aircraft Loading, Aircraft
Categories, Bank Angle vs Load/Stall
AVIATION CALCULATIONS 9
Standard Weights, Equivalents, Quick ConversionTable
COMMUNICATIONS AND NAVAIDS 13
Morse Code, Phonetic Alphabet, Navaid Frequencies,
Navaid Reception Altitudes
FLIGHT PLAN AND WEATHER BRIEFING 15
Special Equipment Suffixes, Transponder Codes,
METAR/TAF, FA, FD, Sigmets, Airmets, TWEB,
NOTAMs, Quick Weather Decoder, High Altitude
Enroute Flight Advisory Service, Turbulence Reports,
Icing Reports, PIREP's
Weather Contractions.. 22
CHECKLISTS **24**
VFR FLIGHT RULES **27**
NTSB 830.. 32
NASA Aviation Safety Reporting System 33
FAR 43 Preventive Maintenance............................ 33
INSTRUMENT FLIGHT RULES **34**
FAR PART 135 .... **43**
EMERGENCIES **47**
Engine Failures, Emergency Communications, Fire,
Medical Conditions, Survival, ELT, Ditching,
Ground to Air Rescue Signals............................... 52
Wind Chill Factor 53
AVIATION ACRONYMS **54**
ICAO Airport Identifier Prefix............................. 59
International Civil Aircraft Markings...................... 60
World Time Zones 62
Frequency Spectrum.. 63
VOR Test Frequencies (VOT) 64
Standard Atmosphere 65
MACH to True Airspeed 66
V-Speeds **67**
AVIATION ABBREVIATIONS **68**
Index 82

(iii)

NAVIGATION AND PERFORMANCE

AIR NAVIGATION FORMULAS

TC ± WCA = TH ± VAR = MH ± DEV = CH
True Course ± Wind Correction Angle = True Heading ± Variation
= Magnetic Heading ± Deviation = Compass Heading

True Course ± Variation = Course Heading TC ± VAR = CH
(Add Westerly Variation, Subtract Easterly Variation)

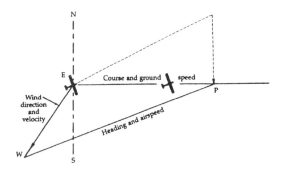

DISTANCE = GROUNDSPEED X TIME

$$TIME = \frac{DISTANCE}{GROUNDSPEED} \qquad GROUNDSPEED = \frac{DISTANCE}{TIME}$$

Nautical Miles per Minute = GS/60
Convert Hours to Minutes = Hours X 60
Convert Minutes to Hours = Minutes/60
(6 minutes = 0.1 hour)

Ground Speed Estimate: Take the distance traveled in 36 seconds and multiply by 100 (3600 seconds = 1 hour)

PILOTAGE/DEAD RECKONING

1. Plot the course on the sectional chart.
2. Add or subtract magnetic variation to determine true course.
3. Determine the angle between the forecast winds (reported in angle from north) and the true course.
4. Using Table 1, add or subtract the headwind or tailwind component to the true airspeed to determine ground speed.

	Table 1 Wind Angle to True Course							
	Headwind-Tailwind Component / Crosswind Component							
	10°	20°	30°	40°	50°	60°	70°	80°
10	10/2	9/3	9/5	8/6	6/8	5/9	3/9	2/10
20	20/3	19/7	17/10	15/13	13/15	10/17	7/19	3/20
30	30/5	28/10	26/15	23/19	19/23	15/26	10/28	5/30
40	39/7	38/14	35/20	31/26	26/31	20/35	14/38	7/39
50	49/9	47/17	43/25	38/32	32/38	25/43	17/47	9/49
60	59/10	56/21	52/30	46/39	39/46	30/52	21/56	10/59
70	69/12	66/24	61/35	54/45	45/54	35/61	24/66	12/69
80	79/14	75/27	69/40	61/51	51/61	40/69	27/75	14/79
90	89/16	85/31	78/45	69/58	58/69	78/45	31/85	16/89
100	98/17	94/34	87/50	77/64	64/77	87/50	94/34	17/98

For winds greater than 100 knots add components

5. Using Table 2, add or subtract the crab angle required to determine compass heading.

TAS	Table 2 Crosswind Component											
	Wind Correction Angle Required (Crab)											
	5	10	15	20	25	30	35	40	45	50	55	60
80	4°	7°	11°	14°	18°	22°	26°	30°	34°	39°	43°	49°
100	3°	6°	9°	12°	14°	17°	20°	24°	27°	30°	33°	37°
120	2°	5°	7°	10°	12°	14°	17°	19°	22°	25°	27°	30°
140	2°	4°	6°	8°	10°	12°	14°	17°	19°	21°	23°	25°
160	2°	4°	5°	7°	9°	11°	13°	15°	16°	18°	20°	22°
180	2°	3°	5°	6°	8°	10°	11°	13°	14°	16°	18°	19°
200	1°	3°	4°	6°	7°	9°	10°	12°	13°	14°	16°	17°
220	1°	3°	4°	5°	7°	8°	9°	10°	12°	13°	14°	16°
240	1°	2°	4°	5°	6°	7°	8°	10°	11°	12°	13°	14°
260	1°	2°	3°	4°	6°	7°	8°	9°	10°	11°	12°	13°
280	1°	2°	3°	4°	5°	6°	7°	8°	9°	10°	11°	12°

For wind components over 60 knots add wind correction angles

PILOTAGE/DEAD RECKONING

6. If the crab angle required is 10° or greater, subtract the groundspeed loss due to crabing. (Table 3)

TAS	Table 3 Wind Correction Angle (Crab)								
	Ground Speed Loss Due to Crabbing								
	10°	15°	20°	25°	30°	35°	40°	45°	50°
80	-1	-3	-5	-7	-11	-14	-19	-23	-29
100	-2	-3	-6	-9	-13	-18	-23	-29	-36
120	-2	-4	-7	-11	-16	-22	-28	-35	-43
140	-2	-5	-8	-13	-19	-25	-33	-41	-50
160	-2	-5	-10	-15	-21	-29	-37	-47	-57
180	-3	-6	-11	-17	-24	-33	-42	-53	-64
200	-3	-7	-12	-19	-27	-36	-47	-59	-71
220	-3	-7	-13	-21	-29	-40	-51	-64	-79
240	-4	-8	-14	-22	-32	-43	-56	-70	-86
260	-4	-9	-16	-24	-35	-47	-61	-76	-93
280	-4	-10	-17	-26	-38	-51	-66	-82	-100
300	-5	-10	-18	-28	-40	-54	-70	-88	-107
320	-5	-10	-19	-30	-43	-58	-75	-94	-114
340	-5	-12	-21	-32	-46	-61	-80	-100	-121

For TAS greater than 280 knots add ground speed losses

RULE OF SIXTY DISTANCE/HEADING CORRECTIONS

To determine distance off course, degrees off course and heading corrections use the One in Sixty Rule: One Degree Off Course at 60 NM Equals 1 NM Off Course.

$$\frac{\text{NM Off Course}}{\text{Distance Flown}} = \frac{\text{Degrees Off Course}}{60}$$

$$\text{Degrees Off Course} = \frac{\text{NM Off Course X 60}}{\text{Distance Flown}}$$

For example 2NM off course in 30 NM would equal 4° off course. A heading correction of 4° will parallel the original course. A heading correction of 8° will intercept the original course in another 30 NM.

SINGLE LINE OF POSITION

Where fuel or daylight may be running short and the destination airport lies along a river, coastline, highway or VOR radial:
1. At a point before reaching the ETA, make a deliberate turn off course.
2. When reaching the coastline, river or VOR radial, turn in the known direction to the destination.

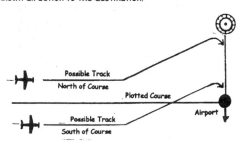

RUNNING FIX

A running fix may be established using two separate LOP's (Line of Position).
1. Note the time crossing the first LOP.
2. When another LOP is crossed note that time and calculate the distance.
3. Advance the first LOP the estimated distance and establish a fix.

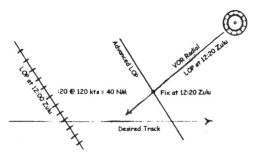

CROSSWIND/HEADWIND COMPONENT CHART

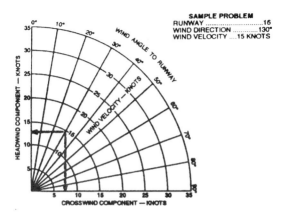

PRESSURE ALTITUDE CONVERSION			
ALTIMETER SETTING (INCHES HG.)	ALTITUDE CORRECTION (FEET)	ALTIMETER SETTING (INCHES HG.)	ALTITUDE CORRECTION (FEET)
28.0	+1,825	29.6	+300
28.1	+1,725	29.7	+205
28.2	+1,630	29.8	+110
28.3	+1,535	29.9	+20
28.4	+1,435	29.92	0
28.5	+1,340	30.0	-75
28.6	+1,245	30.1	-165
28.7	+1,150	30.2	-257
28.8	+1,050	30.3	-350
28.9	+955	30.4	-440
29.0	+865	30.5	-530
29.1	+770	30.6	-620
29.2	+675	30.7	-710
29.3	+580	30.8	-805
29.4	+485	30.9	-895
29.5	+390	31.0	-965

FIELD ELEVATION ± ALTITUDE CORRECTION = PRESSURE ALTITUDE

DENSITY ALTITUDE CHART

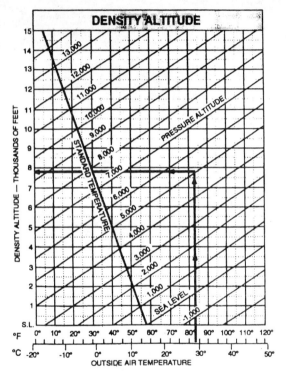

1. Enter Bottom of Chart at OAT
2. Move Up Vertically to Pressure Altitude Diagonal
3. Move Left Horizontal to Read Density Altitude

WEIGHT AND BALANCE

ITEM	WEIGHT		ARM		MOMENT
Aircraft Empty Weight	_____	X	_____	=	_____
Pilot and Front Passenger	_____	X	_____	=	_____
Rear Seat Passengers	_____	X	_____	=	_____
	_____	X	_____	=	_____
Aft Baggage	_____	X	_____	=	_____
Fuel	_____	X	_____	=	_____
TOTAL	_____	X	_____	=	_____

WEIGHT AND BALANCE COMPUTATION
1. Add Weight of Aircraft, Passengers, Baggage, and Fuel.
2. Determine Total Weight to be Within Limits.
3. Multiply Weight by Arm for Moment. (W X A = M)
4. Add Individual Moments for Total Moment.
5. Divide the Total Moment by the Total Weight to Determine the Loaded Center of Gravity. (CG.) (TM/TW = LCG)
6. Determine the Loaded CG. to be Within Limits.

MAXIMUM ALLOWABLE GROSS WEIGHT: _____

CENTER OF GRAVITY LIMITS: FORWARD_____   AFT_____

STANDARD WEIGHTS
1 gallon Jet A = 6.75 lb/3.06 kg
1 liter Jet A = 1.8 lb/0.8 kg
1 gallon Avgas = 6.0 lb.
1 liter Avgas = 1.6 lb./0.719 kg
1 gallon 50W oil = 7.5 lb.
1 quart 50W oil = 1.875 lb.
1 liter 50 W oil = 1.981 lb/0.898 kg
1 gallon water = 8.33 lb.
1 passenger = 170 lb.

WEIGHT AND BALANCE DEFINITIONS
Empty Weight = Aircraft Weight Including Oil and Unusable Fuel
Useful Load = The Weight of Passengers, Usable Fuel, & Baggage
Center of Gravity = The Point of Balance
Datum = A Selected Point on the Longitudinal Axis from which all horizontal measurements are taken.
Arm = The distance between the object and the datum.
Moment = The weight of the object multiplied by the arm.
Gross Weight = Empty Weight plus the Useful Load

WEIGHT SHIFT FORMULA

$$\frac{\text{TOTAL WEIGHT}}{\text{WEIGHT SHIFTED}} = \frac{\text{DISTANCE WEIGHT SHIFTED}}{\text{DISTANCE CG SHIFTED}}$$

MEAN AERODYNAMIC CHORD (MAC)
MAC - Established by the Manufacturer defined as the distance between forward station (LEMAC) and aft station.
CG in % MAC defined as the %MAC distance aft of LEMAC

$$\text{C.G. IN \% MAC} = \frac{\text{CG DISTANCE AFT OF LEMAC}}{\text{MAC}}$$

C.G. Inches From Datum = MAC X % MAC = + LEMAC

AIRCRAFT LOADING
Aft Loaded Aircraft - Unstable pitch, poor stall recovery, higher cruise speed and better fuel economy.
Extreme Aft C.G. - Very unstable, unable to recover from stall/spin condition.
Forward Loaded Aircraft - Stable pitch, lower cruise speed, more elevator down force required.
Extreme Forward C.G. - Unable to flare during landing, nose wheel contacts runway before main wheels.
Over Maximum Gross Weight - Possible structural failure in-flight if severe turbulence or excessive load factors are encountered. Longer takeoff and landing distances, reduced climb performance and higher stall speeds.

AIRCRAFT CATEGORIES	Positive G's	Negative G's
Normal Category (non-acrobatic)	3.8	-1.5
Utility Category (limited acrobatic)	4.4	-1.76
Acrobatic	6.0	-2.4

BANK ANGLE VS INCREASE IN G-FORCE/STALL SPEED

Angle	G-Force	Stall Speed
10°	1.02	$1.02 \times V_s$
20°	1.03	$1.06 \times V_s$
30°	1.15	$1.07 \times V_s$
40°	1.3	$1.14 \times V_s$
50°	1.5	$1.24 \times V_s$
60°	2.0	$1.4 \times V_s$
70°	2.9	$1.7 \times V_s$
80°	5.7	$2.4 \times V_s$
90°	Infinite	Infinite

Maneuvering Speed Approximately = $1.7 \ V_{SO}$

AVIATION CALCULATIONS

1. Time = Distance ÷ Ground Speed: T = D/GS
2. Distance = Time X Ground Speed: D = T X GS
3. Ground Speed = Distance ÷ Time: GS = D/T
4. Nautical Miles per Minute = GS/60
5. Convert Hours to Minutes = Hours X 60
6. Convert Minutes to Hours = Minutes/60
7. Fahrenheit = Celsius X 1.8 + 32: F° = 1.8C° + 32
8. Celsius = (Fahrenheit-32) X 0.56: C° = (F°-32) X 5/9
9. Standard Temperature (ISA) = 15C° - 2 X Altitude/1000: ISA = 15°-2A/1000
10. Gallons per Hour = Gallons Used ÷ Time: GPH = GU/T
11. Time Remaining = Gallons on Board ÷ Gallons per Hour: TR = GOB/GPH
12. Gallons Required = Time X Gallons per Hour: GR = T X GPH
13. Range = Ground Speed X Time Remaining: R = GS X TR
14. Vertical Speed = Altitude Change ÷ Time: VS = AC/T
15. Time to Climb = Altitude Change/Vertical Speed: TTC = A/VS
16. Rate of Climb Required = NM per minute X climb gradient: ROC = NM/MIN X CG
17. Center of Gravity = Total Moment ÷ Total Weight: CG = TM/TW
18. Moment = Weight X Arm: M = W X A
19. Weight Shifted/Total Weight = Distance CG Shifted/Distance Weight Shifted
20. Miles off Course = Degrees Off Course X Distance Flown ÷ 60: MOC = DOC X DF/60
21. Degrees to Intercept = Miles Off Course X 60 ÷ Distance to Fly: DTI = MOC X 60/DTF
22. Degrees off Course = Miles Off Course X 60 ÷ Distance Flown: DOC = MOC X 60/DF
23. Time to Station: (Elapsed Time X 60) ÷ Bearing Change.
24. Distance to Station = (Elapsed Time X Groundspeed)/Bearing Change
25. Vertical Speed = Altitude Change/Time
26. Density Altitude = Pressure Altitude + 120(OAT - ISA)
27. Rate of Climb Required = Feet/NM X Groundspeed/60
28. Hours Decimal = Hours + Minutes/60
29. Hours Minutes = Hours + (Decimal X 60)
30. Center of Gravity = Total Moment/Total Weight
31. Moment = Weight X Arm
32. Weight Shifted/Total Weight = Distance CG Shifted/Distance Weight Shifted
33. Time to Climb = Altitude Change/Vertical Speed
34. Excess Horse Power = (SL Rate of Climb X Gross Weight) ÷ 33,000

35. Rate of Climb = (Excess Horse Power X 33,000) ÷ Actual Weight
36. Rate of Climb = (Gross Weight/Actual Weight)^2 X SL Rate of Climb
37. Specific Range = Nautical Miles/Pounds of Fuel
38. Specific Range = KTAS/Gallons per Hour
39. Specific Endurance = Flight Hours/Pounds of Fuel
40. Specific Endurance = 1/Gallons per Hour
41. Turning Radius = (Velocity/30)/2π
42. Tire Hydroplaning Speed = $9\sqrt{\text{Tire Pressure(PSI)}}$
43. The radius of a standard rate turn in NM is equal to the TAS/200.
44. The radius of a standard rate turn in meters is equal to the TAS times 10.
45. G-force = 1/cosine of the Bank Angle
46. Stall Speed = V_{S1} X $\sqrt{G - \text{Force}}$
47. Less than Gross Weight V_A =

$$V_A\sqrt{\text{Actual Weight / Gross Weight}}$$

48. Pivotal Altitude = TAS(mph)^2/15
49. DME Arc Distance = Degrees of Arc X ($2\pi R$/360)
50. VOR Range NM = $1.23\sqrt{\text{Altitude in Feet}}$
51. Wind Correction Angle(WCA) = (Wind Velocity/NM per Minute) X sine of Wind Angle.
52. Ground Speed Loss Due to Crabbing = TAS - (cosWCA-TAS)

NUMERICAL PREFIXES
nano (n) = .000000001 or 10-9
micro (μ) = .000001 or 10-6
milli = .001 or 10-3
centi (c) = .01 or 10-2
deci (d) = .1 or 10-1
deka (da) = 10 or 101
hecto (h) = 100 or 102
kilo (k) = 1,000 or 103
mega (M) = 1,000,000 or 106
giga (G) = 1,000,000,000 or 109

METRIC MEASURES
1 meter = 1,000 millimeters or 100 centimeters
1 kilometer = 1,000 meters
1 liter = 1,000 milliliters
1 kiloliters = 1,000 liters
1 gram = 1,000 milligrams
1 kilogram = 1,000 grams
1 metric ton = 1,000 kilograms

STANDARD WEIGHTS
1 gallon Jet A = 6.75 lb/3.06 kg
1 liter Jet A = 1.8 lb/0.8 kg
1 gallon Avgas = 6.0 lb/2.72 kg
1 liter Avgas = 1.6 lb./0.719 kg
1 gallon 50W oil = 7.5 lb/3.4 kg
1 quart 50W oil = 1.875 lb/0.85 kg
1 liter 50 W oil = 1.981 lb/0.898 kg
1 gallon water = 8.33 lb.
1 gallon methanol = 6.62 lb.
1 passenger = 170 lb.

EQUIVALENTS
1 inch mercury = 33.863 millibars or hectopascals
1 millibar or hectopascal = 0.02953 inches of mercury
1 millimeter hg = 1.332 millibars or hectopascals
1 meter per second = 196.85 feet per minute
1 meter per second = 1.9438 nautical miles per hour
1 foot per second = 60 feet per minute = 3,600 feet per hour
1 statute mile/hour = 88 feet per minute = 1.46 feet per second
1 nautical mile/hour = 101.2 feet per minute = 1.68 feet per sec.
1 kilogram = 2.2046 pounds
1 pound = .45359 kilograms
1 kilometer = .62137 statute miles or .53996 NM
1 statute mile = .86898 NM or 1.6093 kilometers or 5280 feet
1 nautical mile = 6076 feet
1 nautical mile = 1.15 statute miles or 1.852 kilometers
1 foot = .3048 meters
1 meter = 3.2808 feet or 1.0936 yards
1 yard = .9144 meters
1 inch = 25.4 millimeters (mm)
1 square inch = 6.5 square centimeters
1 cubic inch = 16 cubic centimeters
1 US gallon = 3.7853 liters or .83267 Imperial gallons
1 US gallon = 231 cubic inches or 0.134 cubic feet
1 liter = .26418 US gallons
1' (minute) latitude(N/S) = 1 nautical mile
1' (minute) longitude (E/W) = 1 NM(cosine latitude)
1 kHz = 1,000 Hertz, 1 MHz = 1,000,000 Hertz or 1,000 kHz

ICAO SEA LEVEL AIR STANDARD VALUES
Pressure = 1013 Mb = 760 mm Hg = 14.7 psi
Temperature = 15° C = 59° F
Speed of Sound = 741.4 miles per hour or 1087.4 feet per second

AERONAUTICAL CHART SCALES
Terminal Area - 4 SM or 3.5 NM per inch
Sectional - 8 SM or 7 NM per inch
WAC and ONC - 16 SM or 14 NM per inch

QUICK CONVERSION TABLE

Convert From	Into	Multiply By
Nautical Miles	Statute Miles	1.1508
	Feet	6076.1
	Kilometers	1.852
	Meters	1852
Statute Miles	Nautical Miles	0.86898
	Feet	5280.0
	Kilometers	1.6094
	Meters	1609.344
Meters	Feet	3.2808
	Yards	1.0936
	Statute Miles	0.000621
	Nautical Miles	0.000539
Kilometers	Statute Miles	0.62136
	Nautical Miles	0.53995
	Feet	3280.8
U.S. Gallons	Liters	3.7854
	AV Gas lb.	6.0
	Jet A lb.	6.75
	Jet A kg	3.06
	Oil lb	7.5
	Oil kg	3.4
US Quarts	Liters	0.946335
	Oil lb	1.875
	US Gallons	0.25
Liters	US Quarts	1.0567
	U.S. Gallons	0.26417
	AV Gas lb	1.58
	AV Gas kg	0.719
	Jet A lb	1.8
	Jet A kg	0.8
	Oil lb	1.9813
	Oil kg	0.89871
US Pounds	Kilograms	0.45359
	Jet A Gallons	0.148148
	Jet A Liters	0.55555
	AV Gas Gallons	0.166667
	AV Gas Liters	0.63291
	Oil Gallons	1.33333
	Oil Liters	0.5047
Kilograms	US Pounds	2.2046
	Jet A Gallons	0.32904
	Jet A Liters	1.25
	AV Gas Gallons	0.36743
	AV Gas Liters	1.3908
	Oil Gallons	0.29395
	Oil Quarts	1.1758

COMMUNICATIONS AND NAVAIDS

118.0 - 121.4 MHz	Air Traffic Control
121.5 MHz	Emergency, ELT signals
121.6 - 121.9	Airport Ground Control
122.00 MHz	Enroute Flight Advisory Service
122.025 - 122.075 MHz	Flight Service Station FSS
122.1 MHz	FSS Receive Only with VOR
122.125 - 122.175 MHz	FSS
122.2 MHz	FSS Common Enroute Simplex
122.225 - 122.675 MHz	FSS
122.7 MHz	Unicom, Uncontrolled Airports
122.725 MHz	Unicom, Uncontrolled Airports
122.750 MHz	Air to Air, Private Airports, non-public
122.80 MHz	Unicom, Uncontrolled Airports
122.85 MHz	Air to Air, Private Airports, non-public
122.90 MHz	Multicom at Airports with no Control Tower or FSS, Temporary Emergency
122.925 MHz	Multicom Forestry Service
122.95 MHz	Unicom at Airports with Control Tower
122.975 MHz	Unicom, Uncontrolled Airports
123.0 & 123.050 MHz	Unicom - uncontrolled airports
123.025 MHz	Air to Air Helicopters
123.075 MHz	Unicom Uncontrolled Airports
123.10 MHz	Temporary Control, Search and Rescue
123.15 - 123.575 MHz	Flight Test
123.3 & 123.5 MHz	Flight Schools Gliders, Hot Air Balloons
123.6 - 123.65 MHz	FSS on the Airport
123.675 - 128.8 MHz	ATC
128.825 - 132.0 MHz	Aeronautical Enroute ARINC
132.05 - 135.95 MHz	ATC

NAVIGATION AIDS

190 - 544 kHz	Non-directional Beacons (NDB's), ILS Compass Locators
75 MHz	Fan Markers, Z Markers, ILS Markers
108.1 - 111.9 MHz	ILS Localizers - odd tenths
108.2 - 111.8 MHz	Terminal VOR's - even tenths
112.0 - 117.9 MHz	VOR's

NDB RECEPTION RANGE

Compass Locator	
25 Watts	15 NM
MH 50 Watts	25 NM
H 50 - 1999 Watts	50 NM
HH 2,000 + Watts	75 NM

VOR STANDARD SERVICE VOLUMES

Class Navaid	Altitude	Distance
Terminal VOR	to 12,000' MSL	25 NM
Low Altitude VOR	to 18,000' MSL	40 NM
High Altitude VOR	to 18,000' MSL	40 NM
High Altitude VOR	14,500' to 18,000' MSL	100 NM
High Altitude VOR	18,000' to FL 450	130 NM
High Altitude VOR	above FL 450	100 NM
DME Reception	Line of Sight	199 NM

LINE OF SIGHT VOR RECEPTION

Altitude Above VOR	Line of Sight
500'	27 NM
1,000'	39 NM
2,000'	55 NM
3,000'	67 NM
5,000'	87 NM
7,000'	103 NM
10,000'	123 NM

Altitude (NM) = $1.23 \sqrt{\text{Altitude in Feet}}$

VOR IDENTIFICATION

Morse Code Identification 6 to 8 times per minute
Voice Identification - Name of Range followed by the word "VOR"
DME Identification Broadcast approximately every 30 seconds.

MORSE CODE/TELEPHONY

• –	A	ALPHA	–	T	TANGO
– • • •	B	BRAVO	• • –	U	UNIFORM
– • – •	C	CHARLIE	• • • –	V	VICTOR
– • •	D	DELTA	• – –	W	WHISKEY
•	E	ECHO	– • • –	X	X-RAY
• • – •	F	FOXTROT	– • – –	Y	YANKEE
– – •	G	GOLF	– – • •	Z	ZULU
• • • •	H	HOTEL	• – – – –	1	WUN
• •	I	INDIA	• • – – –	2	TOO
• – – –	J	JULIET	• • • – –	3	TREE
– • –	K	KILO	• • • • –	4	FOW-ER
• – • •	L	LIMA	• • • • •	5	FIFE
– –	M	MIKE	– • • • •	6	SIX
– •	N	NOVEMBER	– – • • •	7	SEV-EN
– – –	O	OSCAR	– – – • •	8	AIT
• – – •	P	PAPA	– – – – •	9	NIN-ER
– – • –	Q	QUEBEC	– – – – –	0	ZEE-RO
• – •	R	ROMEO	• • • • • • • •		ERROR
• • •	S	SIERRA	• – • – • –		END MESSAGE

FLIGHT PLAN AND WEATHER BRIEFING

FLIGHT SERVICE 1-800-WX-BRIEF (992-7433)
GTE DUATS 1-800-767-9989 Voice:1-800-345-3828
DTC DUATS 1-800-245-3828 Voice: 1-800-243-3828

WX BRIEFING FORMAT
Adverse Conditions.
Synopsis.
Current Weather/PIREPS.
Enroute Forecast.
Destination Forecast.
Winds and Temperatures Aloft.
Notams.

FLIGHT PLAN SEQUENCE
1. Type of Plan VFR or IFR.
2. Aircraft Identification.
3. Aircraft Type and Special Equipment.
4. True Airspeed.
5. Departure Point.
6. Time of Departure.
7. Cruising Altitude.
8. Route of Flight.
9. Destination Airport and City.
10. Estimated Time Enroute.
11. Remarks.
12. Fuel on Board.
13. Alternate Airports.
14. Pilot's Information. Aircraft Home Base.
15. Number of Persons On Board.
16. Color of Aircraft.

SPECIAL EQUIPMENT SUFFIXES
/U Transponder - Mode C
/T Transponder - no Mode C
/X No Transponder
/A DME-Transponder - Mode C
/B DME-Transponder - no Mode C
/D DME- no Transponder
/I RNAV, LORAN, VOR/DME - Mode C
/E Dual FMS and IRU - Mode C
/Q RVSM/RNP - Mode C
/G GPS - En route and Approach Capability - Mode C

TRANSPONDER CODES

1200	VFR	7500	Hijack
7700	Emergency	7600	Lost Communications

(15)

METAR Aviation Routine Weather Report Scheduled hourly observation. SPECI indicates special report.

METAR KPIT 201955Z 22015G25KT 3/4SM 28R/2600FT TSRA OVC010CB 18/16 A2992 RMK RETSB23

Decoded Report - Pittsburgh International Airport, 20th day of the month, 1955 UTC, wind 220 at 15 knots, gusts to 25 knots, visibility 3/4 **statute mile**, runway 28 right RVR is 2600', **thunderstorms** and **moderate rain**, 1,000 foot overcast clouds consisting of **cumulonimbus** clouds, temperature 18° Celsius, dewpoint 16° Celsius, altimeter setting 29.92". ReMarKs: REcent weather event ThunderStorm Began 23 minutes past the hour.

TAF Terminal Aerodrome Forecast: Contains a definitive forecast for specific time periods.

TAF KPIT 091720Z 091818 22020KT 3SM SHRA BKN020

FM2030 30015G25KT WS015/30045KT 3SM SHRA OVC015
PROB40 2022 1/2 TSRA OVC008CB

FM2300 27008KT 5SM -SHRA BKN020 OVC040 TEMPO 0407
0000KT 1SM -RA FG

FM1000 22010KT 5SM -SHRA OVC020 BECMG 1315 20010KT
P6SM NSW SKC

Decoded Forecast: Pittsburgh International Airport, 9th day of the month, 1720 UTC, valid from 1800Z of the 9th to 1800Z of the next day, wind 220° at 20 knots, 3 statute miles visibility, moderate rain showers, broken clouds at 2,000'.

WS015/30045KT means at 1500 feet we expect wind to be 300 degrees at 45 knots. This indicates low level wind shear, not associated with convective activity.

FM2030 means From 2030Z (UTC time).

PROB040 means there is a **40% probability** of the condition between 2000Z and 2200Z.

TEMPO 0407 means **Temporary** changes expected between 0400Z and 0700Z.

BECMG 1315 means conditions **Becoming** as described between 1300Z and 1500Z.

(16)

METAR/TAF CODES & DEFINITIONS

A01 Automated Observation ASOS/AWOS without precipitation discriminator (reportable rain/snow)

A02 Automated Observation ASOS/AWOS with precipitation discriminator (rain/snow)

A2992 US altimeter setting reported in inches of mercury

AMD Amended Forecast (TAF)

AUTO Only a fully automated site without human intervention will contain the word AUTO.

BECMG Becoming (expected between 2 digit beginning and 2 digit ending hour)

CAVOK CEILING AND VISIBILITY OKAY

CAVU CEILING & VISIBILITY UNLIMITED, 10+ miles

CLR Clear at or below 12,000 feet (ASOS/AWOS report)

COR Correction to the observation

DSNT Distant: Phenomena beyond 10 statute miles.

FROPA Frontal Passage.

FM From (4 digit beginning time in hours and minutes)

M In temperature field means "minus" or below zero, In RVR indicates visibility less than lowest sensor value

NO Not available (e.g. SLPNO, RVRNO)

NSW No significant weather Note: NSW only indicates obstruction to visibility or precipitation previously noted has ended. Low ceilings, wind shear, other conditions may still exist.

P In RVR indicates visibility greater than highest reportable sensor value (e.g. P6000FT)

P6SM Visibility greater than 6 SM (TAF only)

PK WND Peak wind over 25 knots will be added to remarks section.

PROB40 Probability 40 percent

Q1013 International altimeter setting reported in hectopascals

SLP Sea Level Pressure (e.g. 1013 reported as 013)

TEMPO Temporary changes expected (between 2 digit beginning 2 digit ending hour)

VC Vicinity: Between 5 and 10 statute miles.

VRB Variable wind direction when speed is 6 knots or less.

VV Vertical Visibility (Indefinite Ceiling)

WS Wind Shear (In TAFs, low level and not associated with convective activity

WSHFT Windshift reported in remarks section. WSHFT 30 FROPA "Wind shift at 30 due to frontal passage.

AREA FORECAST (FA) are 12-hour aviation forecasts plus a 6-hour categorical outlook and are issued 3 times / day. Area forecasts cover an area the size of several states and comprise 5 sections: HAZARDS/FLIGHT PRECAUTIONS (H), ICING (I), SYNOPSIS (S), TURBULENCE (T) (and LOW LEVEL WIND SHEAR if applicable), and SIGNIFICANT CLOUDS AND WEATHER (C).

WINDS AND TEMPERATURES ALOFT FORECASTS (FD) are 6, 12, and 24-hour forecasts of wind direction (nearest 10° true) and speed (knots) for selected flight levels. Forecast Temperatures Aloft (°C) are included for all but the 3000-foot level. Example:

FD WBC 121645
BASED ON 121200Z DATA VALID 130000Z FOR USE 2100-0600Z. TEMPS NEG ABV 24000 FT

	3000	6000	9000	12000	18000
BOS	3127	3425-07	3420-11	3421-16	3516-27
JFK	3026	3327-08	3324-12	3322-16	3120-27

At 6000 feet over JFK the wind is from 330° at 27 knots and temperature minus 8°C. A coded direction is used for wind speed 100 knots or greater. Example: STL forecast at FL 390 "731960." Wind is 230° (73-50=23) at 119 knots (100 + 19 = 119). The temperature is -60° Celsius.

IN-FLIGHT AVIATION WEATHER ADVISORIES
CONVECTIVE SIGMET (WST) implies severe or greater turbulence, severe icing, and low level wind shear. WSTs are issued for surface winds greater than 50 knots, surface hail 3/4" or greater, tornadoes, numerous or embedded thunderstorms.

SIGMET (WS) advise of weather potentially hazardous to all aircraft other than convective activity. Items covered are, severe icing, severe or extreme turbulence, dust storms, sandstorms, or volcanic ash lowering visibility to less than 3 miles.

AIRMET (WA) advise of weather that may be hazardous to smaller aircraft or VFR only pilots. Items covered are; moderate icing, moderate turbulence, sustained surface winds of more than 30 knots, ceilings less than 1,000 feet and/or visibility of less than 3 miles affecting over 50% of the area at a time, and extensive obscuring of mountains.

CONTINUOUS TRANSCRIBED WEATHER BROADCAST (TWEB) - Individual route forecasts covering a 25-nautical-mile zone either side of the route. By requesting a specific route number, detailed en route weather for a 15-hour period plus a synopsis can be obtained.

NOTICES TO AIRMEN
NOTAM D - Distant Notams, Navigation Equipment, Approach Lights, Frequency Changes
NOTAM L - Local Notams, Taxiway Closures, VASI Out of Service, Personnel Working Near Runways
FDC NOTAM- Flight Data Center, IFR Chart Changes, Temporary Flight Restrictions

QUICK WEATHER DECODER		
CODE	**DEFINITION**	**REMEMBER**
BC	Patches	Bits & Chunks
BL	Blowing	Blowing
BR	Mist ≥ 1/2 mile	Baby Rain
DR	Low Drifting	low Drifting
DU	Dust	Dust
DS	Dust Storm	Dust Storm
DZ	Drizzle	DriZZle
FC	Funnel Cloud	Funnel Cloud
FG	Fog ≤ 1/2 mile	FoG
FU	Smoke	Fumes
FZ	Freezing	FreeZing
GR	Hail	Granite Rain
GS	Small Hail	Granite Small
HZ	Haze	HaZe
IC	Ice Crystals	Ice Crystals
MI	Shallow	MInimal
PE	Pellets	Pellets
PO	Dust/sand Whirls	sand POckets
PR	Partial	PaRtial
PY	Spray	sPraY
RA	Rain	RAin
SA	Sand	SAnd
SG	Snow Grains	Snow Grains
SH	Showers	SHowers
SN	Snow	SNow
SQ	Squall	SQuall
SS	Sand Storm	Sand Storm
TS	Thunderstorm	ThunderStorm
UP	Unknown	Unknown Precipitation
VA	Volcanic Ash	Volcanic Ash
SKC	Clear	0
CLR	Clear	0
FEW	Few Clouds	1/8 - 2/8
SCT	Scattered	3/8 - 4/8
BKN	Broken	5/8 - 7/8
OVC	Overcast	8/8
VV	Vertical Visibility	8/8
CB	Cumulonimbus	CumulonimBus
TCU	Towering Cumulus	Towering CUmulus

HIGH ALTITUDE ENROUTE FLIGHT ADVISORY SERVICE FREQUENCIES (FLIGHT WATCH)

Albuquerque	127.625	Kansas City	128.475
Albuquerque	134.825	Los Angeles	135.900
Atlanta	135.475	Memphis	133.675
Boston	133.925	Miami	132.725
Chicago	134.875	Minneapolis	135.675
Cleveland	135.425	New York	134.725
Denver	124.675	Oakland	135.700
Fort Worth	133.775	Salt Lake City	133.025
Houston	126.625	Seattle	135.925
Indianapolis	134.825	Washington	134.525
Jacksonville	134.175		

FLIGHT WATCH BELOW FL180 122.0 MHz

TURBULENCE REPORTING CRITERIA

Light Turbulence - Momentarily causes slight erratic changes in attitude and or altitude. Slight strain against seatbelts.

Light Chop - Causes slight rapid rhythmic bumpiness without changes to altitude or attitude. Slight strain against seatbelts.

Moderate Turbulence - Changes in altitude and attitude. Aircraft remains in positive control. Small variations in IAS. Definite strain against seatbelts.

Moderate Chop - Rapid bumps or jolts without appreciable changes in to altitude/attitude. Definite strain against seatbelts.

Severe Turbulence - Causes large abrupt changes to altitude and altitude. Large variations in IAS. Aircraft may be momentarily out of control. Occupants violently force against seat belts.

Extreme Turbulence - Aircraft is violently tossed about and almost impossible to control.

Occasional - Less than 1/3 of the time.

Intermittent - 1/3 to 2/3 of the time.

Continuous - More than 2/3 of the time.

ICING REPORTING CRITERIA

Trace - Ice becomes perceptible. Rate of accumulation slow. Not hazardous even though deicing/anti-icing equipment is not used unless encountered for an extended period of time, over one hour.

Light - Rate of accumulation may create a problem is flight is prolonged under these conditions, over one hour. Occasional use of deicing/anti-icing equipment removes/prevents accumulation.

Moderate - The rate of accumulation is such that even short encounters become potentially hazardous. The use of deicing/anti-icing equipment or diversion is necessary.

Severe - The rate of accumulation is such that deicing/anti-icing equipment fails to reduce or control the hazard. Immediate diversion is necessary.

ICE DESCRIPTIONS
Rime Ice - Rough milky opaque ice formed by the instantaneous freezing of small super cooled water droplets.
Clear Ice - A glossy clear of translucent ice formed by the relatively slow freezing of large supercooled water droplets.
Mixed Ice - A combination of rime and clear ice.

PILOT REPORTS (PIREPs)
UA	Pilot Report
UUA	Urgent Pilot Report
/OV	Location:
/TM	Time:
/FL	Altitude/Flight level:
/TP	Aircraft Type:
/SK	Sky Cover:
/WX	Flight Visibility and Weather:
/TA	Temperature (Celsius):
/WV	Wind:
/TB	Turbulence:
/IC	Icing:
/RM	Remarks:

AWOS - AUTOMATED WEATHER OBSERVING SYSTEM

AWOS-1	Altimeter, wind, temperature/dew point and density altitude
AWOS-2	AWOS-1 information plus visibility
AWOS-3	AWOS-2 information plus clouds/ceiling

ASOS - AUTOMATED SURFACE OBSERVING SYSTEM

ASOS reports will contain the following information: type of report, station identifier, date/time, report modifier (AUTO with no human intervention), wind direction and speed, visibility, runway visual range, weather phenomena, sky condition, temperature/dew point, altimeter, remarks.

AO1 in the remarks section indicates an automated station without a precipitation discriminator.
AO2 in the remarks section indicates an automated station with a precipitation discriminator. A precipitation discriminator can determine the difference between liquid and frozen/freezing precipitation.

WEATHER CONTRACTIONS

+	HEAVY, INCREASING	CCSL	STANDING LENTICULAR CIRROCUMULUS
++	VERY HEAVY		
-	LIGHT, THIN, DECREASING	CDFNT	COLD FRONT
--	VERY LIGHT	CFP	COLD FRONT PASSAGE
X	INTENSE	CI	CIRRUS
XX	EXTREME	CIG	CEILING
( )	NO SIGN - MODERATE	CLRS	CLEAR AND SMOOTH
0000KT	WIND CALM	CNVG	CONVERGE
99	VISIBILITY GREATER THAN 7 MILES	CS	CIRROSTRATUS
		CU	CUMULUS
9900	LIGHT AND VARIABLE	CUFRA	CUMULUS FRACTUS
		CW	CLOCKWISE
		DABRK	DAYBREAK
AC	ALTOCUMULUS	DALGT	DAYLIGHT
ACCAS	ALTOCUMULUS CASTELLANUS	DFUS	DIFFUSE
		DNSLP	DOWNSLOPE
ACLD	ABOVE CLOUDS	DTRT	DETERIORATE
ACSL	STANDING LENTICULAR ALTOCUMULUS	DURC	DURING CLIMB
		DURG	DURING
		DURGC	DURING CLIMB
ACYC	ANTICYCLONIC	DURGD	DURING DESCENT
ADVCTN	ADVECTION	E	ENDING PRECIPITATION
ALF	ALOFT	EMBDD	EMBEDDED
ALG	ALONG	FC	FRACTOCUMULUS
ALQDS	ALL QUADRANTS	FNTGNS	FRONTOGENESIS (FRONT FORMING)
ALSEC	ALL SECTORS		
ALSTG	ALTIMETER SETTING	FNTLYS	FRONTOLYSIS
AOA	AT OR ABOVE	FR	FALLING RAPIDLY
AOB	AT OR BELOW	FRA	FRACTUS CLOUDS
AS	ALTOSTRATUS	FROPA	FRONTAL PASSAGE
BCOB	BROKEN CLOUDS OR BETTER	FRZLVL	FREEZING LEVEL
		G	GUSTS
BFDK	BEFORE DARK	GFDEP	GROUND FOG EST. DEPTH (FEET)
BINOVC	BREAKS IN OVERCAST		
BLO	BELOW (PIREP)	HYR	HIGHER
BOVC	BASE OF OVERCAST	ICG	ICING
BRAF	BRAKING ACTION FAIR	ICGIC	ICING IN CLOUDS
BRAG	BRAKING ACTION GOOD	ICGICIP	ICING IN CLOUDS AND IN PRECIPITATION
BRAN	BRAKING ACTION NIL		
BRAP	BRAKING ACTION POOR	ICGIP	ICING IN PRECIPITATION
BRKHIC	BREAKS IN HIGHER OVERCAST		
		INTMT	INTERMITTENT
CAS	CASTELLANUS	INVOF	IN VICINITY OF
CAT	CLEAR AIR TURBULENCE	INVRN	INVERSION
CBMAM	CUMULONIMBUS MAMA	IPV	IMPROVE
CC	CIRROCUMULUS	JTSTR	JETSTREAM
		KMH	KILOMETERS/HOUR

(22)

LLWS	LOW LEVEL WIND SHEAR	RE	RECENT WEATHER EVENT
LTG	LIGHTNING	RMK	REMARK
LTGCA	LIGHTNING CLOUD-TO-AIR	RTD	ROUTINE DELAYED WEATHER
LTGCC	LIGHTNING CLOUD-TO-CLOUD	RVRM	RVR AT MIDPOINT
		RVRNO	RVR NOT AVAILABLE
LTGCG	LIGHTNING CLOUD-TO-GROUND	RVRR	RVR ON ROLLOUT
		RVRT	RVR AT TOUCHDOWN
LTGCW	LIGHTNING CLOUD-TO-WATER	RVV	RUNWAY VISIBILITY VALUE
LTGIC	LIGHTNING IN CLOUDS	SC	STRATOCUMULUS,
		SCOB	SCATTERED CLOUDS OR BETTER
MEGG	MERGING		
MI	MEDIUM INTENSITY	SCSL	STANDING LENTICULAR STRATOCUMULUS
MLTLVL	MELTING LEVEL		
MOGR	MODERATE OR GREATER	SL	STANDING LENTICULAR
		SLP	SEA LEVEL PRESSURE
NCWX	NO CHANGE IN WEATHER	SLPG	SLOPING
		SP	STATION PRESSURE,
NPRS	NON PERSISTENT	SQLN	SQUALL LINE
NS	NIMBOSTRATUS,	ST	STRATUS
NSC	NO SIGNIFICANT CLOUDS	STFR(A)	STRATUS FRACTUS
		STFRM	STRATIFORM
OAOI	ON & OFF INSTRUMENTS	STS	STRATUS
		TCU	TOWERING CUMULUS
OBSCD	OBSCURED	TKOF	TAKEOFF
OCFNT	OCCLUDED FRONT	TOVC	TOP OF OVERCAST
OCLD	OCCLUDE	TROF	TROUGH
OCLN	OCCLUSION	TROP	TROPOPAUSE
OFP	OCCLUDED FRONTAL PASSAGE	TRPLYR	TRAPPING LAYER
		TRRN	TERRAIN
OI	ON INSTRUMENTS	TRW	THUNDERSHOWER
OMTNS	OVER MOUNTAINS	TSHWR	THUNDERSHOWER
ONSHR	ONSHORE	TSTM(S)	THUNDERSTORM(S)
O/T	OTHER TIMES	U	UNKNOWN INTENSITY
OTAS	ON TOP AND SMOOTH	UDDF	UP AND DOWN DRAFTS
OTP	ON TOP	UP	UNKNOWN PRECIPITATION
PRESFR	PRESSURE FALLING RAPIDLY		
		V	VARIES
PRESRR	PRESSURE RISING RAPIDLY	VSBY	VISIBILITY
		WFP	WARM FRONT PASSAGE
PROG	PROGNOSIS		
PTLY	PARTLY	WH	HURRICANE ADVISORY
QSTNRY	QUASI-STATIONARY	WXR	WEATHER RADAR
R	RUNWAY (RVR)	XPC(D)	EXPECT(ED)
RAREP	RADAR WEATHER REPORT	XTRM	EXTREME

(23)

CHECKLISTS

CROSS-COUNTRY
Sectional Charts.
Aircraft Flight Manual.
Airport Facilities Directory or Airport Guide.
Clipboard and Pencils.
Flight Computer and Plotter.
Airsick Bags.
Warm Clothing.
Flashlight(s)!
Headsets or extra Microphone.
Fuel Tester.
Fire Extinguisher.
Survival Equipment and Water.
Life Jackets (over water).
Pilot's Certificate and Medical Certificate.

AIRCRAFT
A.R.R.O.W.
Aircraft Lights --OPERATIONAL.
Engine Oil -- FULL. Extra quarts if needed.
Tires -- PROPER INFLATION.
Windshield -- CLEAN.
Instrument Panel Lights -- OPERATIONAL.

ROUTE PLANNING
Aircraft Takeoff and Landing Performance.
Fuel Available at Destination and Alternatives.
Weather Briefing.
Flight Plan Filed. Departure and Destination Contacts should know;
Type Aircraft, N-number, Airport Name, FBO, Persons on Board,
Telephone Numbers.
ATC Radar and FSS frequencies along the route.
Altitude/Oxygen Requirements (8,000' night).
Flight Plan Alternatives.

CABIN
Control Locks - REMOVED,
Magnetos-Off
Landing Gear-DOWN
Radios, Avionics Master, Electrical Switches - OFF.
Master Switch - ON.
Fuel Quantity Indicators - CHECK QUANTITY.
Aircraft Lights - CHECK.
Master Switch - OFF.
Fuel Selector Valve - CHECK ON

(24)

EMPENNAGE
Gust Locks - REMOVED.
Anticollision Lights - CHECK.
Control Surfaces - CHECK.

WINGS
Leading and Trailing Edges - CHECK for Damage
Flaps - CHECK security and Alignment
Ailerons -- CHECK
Fuel Sumps - DRAIN.
Wing Tips - CHECK for damage. Navigation lights -- CHECK.
Fuel Quantities - CHECK VISUALLY
Fuel Tank Vents - CHECK
Pitot Tube - REMOVE COVER. Check clear
Stall Indicator - CHECK free and clear.

ENGINE
Engine Oil Level - CHECK. Filler Cap -- SECURE.
Fuel Strainer/Sump - DRAIN.
Battery Mounts and Wiring - CHECK
Manifold/Exhaust - CHECK for cracks/exhaust leaks.
Propeller - CHECK for nicks and blade security.
Spinner -- CHECK for cracks
Oil Cooler/Air Intake - CHECK clear of obstructions.

LANDING GEAR
Tires and Struts - CHECK condition and inflation
Brakes -CHECK condition and fluid leaks.

FUSELAGE
Static Source - CHECK clear
Antennas - CHECK security
Skin - CHECK for damage

STARTING ENGINE
Seat Belts, Shoulder Harnesses - ADJUST.
Avionics Electrical Switches - OFF
Circuit Breakers - CHECK IN.
Brakes - TEST and SET.
Carburetor Heat - OFF.
Cowl Flaps - OPEN
Master Switch -- ON.
Propeller Area - YELL CLEAR.
Follow recommended starting procedure
Oil Pressure - CHECK.
Beacon/Navigation Lights - ON as required.
Avionics Power Switch, Radios - ON.

BEFORE TAKEOFF
Flight Controls -- FREE and CORRECT.
Check Instruments - Altimeter Field Elevation, Directional Gyro
set to compass or runway heading.
Fuel Selector and Pumps - ON
Trims/Flaps - SET for takeoff
Engine Runup - CHECK magnetos each/both, exercise propeller
Doors/Windows - CLOSED.
Seatbelts - SECURE
Approach Area - CLEAR of traffic
Transponder -- ON ALT. Squawk as assigned

ENROUTE
Maintain vigilance for traffic
Fuel Mixture - LEAN as required.
Engine Instruments - CHECK
Check periodically for carburetor icing

BEFORE LANDING
Carburetor Heat - AS REQUIRED
Seat Belts, Shoulder Straps - SECURE
Fuel Selector Valve - ON full tank
Fuel Pumps - AS REQUIRED
Landing Gear - DOWN and LOCKED.
Mixture - RICH.
Propeller - High RPM
Brakes - TEST.

MISSED APPROACH
Power - FULL THROTTLE
Attitude - Climb Pitch
Flaps/Gear - RETRACT as required
Airspeed -BEST CLIMB

POST FLIGHT
Tune to 121.5 - CHECK ELT
Engine Shutdown.
Master Switch - OFF
Magnetos - OFF
Tie-Downs and Wheel Chocks - SECURE.
Control Locks - INSTALLED
Pitot Covers - INSTALLED
Flight Plan - CLOSED

VFR FLIGHT RULES

PILOT CURRENCY REQUIREMENTS
Medical Certificate. Within the previous 24 months for private pilot privileges. (FAR 61.23a, 61.3c)
Flight Review. Within the previous 24 calendar months. (FAR 61.56)
Day Recent Flight Experience – Pilot In Command. To carry passengers within the previous 90 days, 3 takeoffs and landings as the sole manipulator of the flight controls, in the same category and class (single engine, multiengine, etc).
Tailwheel Aircraft. If the aircraft is a tailwheel airplane the landings must be to a full stop in a tailwheel airplane. (FAR 61.57c)
Night Recent Flight Experience – Pilot In Command. To carry passengers at night, three takeoffs and landings to a full stop within the period from one hour after sunset to one hour before sunrise in the same category and class within the previous 90 days.

AIRCRAFT CURRENCY REQUIREMENTS
Annual Inspection. Within the previous 12 calendar months. *The annual inspection is entered in the aircraft maintenance logs and should note the next compliance due of any recurring Airworthiness Directives.* (FAR 91.409)
100 Hour Inspection. Required for aircraft used for hire.
Transponder/Altimeter System Test. Within the previous 24 calendar months. (FAR 91.411, 91.413)
ELT Battery Replacement: Within 24 months or 1 hour cumulative use. Expiration date marked on transmitter and in aircraft maintenance record.
ELT Operational check: Within 12 calendar months and noted in aircraft maintenance record. (FAR 91.207)

AIRCRAFT AIRWORTHINESS 91.7
The owner or operator of the aircraft is responsible for maintaining the aircraft in an airworthy condition. The pilot in command is responsible for determining the aircraft is in condition for a safe flight.

ALCOHOL OR DRUGS 91.17
A pilot may not operate an aircraft within 8 hours after consuming an alcoholic beverage, while using any drug that may affect his ability to fly safely, while having .04 percent by weight or more alcohol in the blood. A pilot may not carry a passenger that appears to be intoxicated.

PREFLIGHT ACTION REQUIRED 91.103

For any flight, the runway lengths of intended use, takeoff and landing performance of the aircraft.

For a flight not in the vicinity of the airport or an IFR flight: Weather reports and forecasts, fuel requirements, alternatives available if the flight cannot be completed as planned, any known traffic delays advised by ATC.

PILOT USE OF SAFETY BELTS 91.105, 91.107

A pilot must wear a safety belt and shoulder harness during takeoff and landing and while seated en route. The pilot must brief the passengers on the use of safety belts and ensure they are fastened before taxiing the aircraft. Child car seats used in airplanes should be labeled, "THIS RESTRAINT IS APPROVED FOR USE IN MOTOR VEHICLES AND AIRCRAFT". The car seat should be secured in a forward facing seat and a person must be designated to attend to the safety of the child during the flight.

FLIGHT OPERATIONS NEAR OTHER AIRCRAFT 91.111

Pilots may not operate an aircraft close to another aircraft as to create a collision hazard. Aircraft may not fly in formation flight unless agreed to by the pilot in command of each aircraft. Aircraft carrying passengers for hire may not fly in formation.

RIGHT-OF-WAY RULES 91.113

In distress. An aircraft in distress has the right of way over all other air traffic.

Converging. When aircraft of the same category are converging at the same altitude (except head-on or nearly so), the aircraft to the others right has the right of way. If the aircraft are of different categories:

A balloon has the right-of-way over any other category. A glider has the right-of-way over an airship, airplane or rotorcraft. An airship has the right-of-way over an airplane or rotorcraft. Towing or refueling aircraft has the right-of-way over all other engine driven aircraft.

Approaching head-on. Aircraft approaching head-on shall alter course to the right.

Overtaking. Aircraft being overtaken have the right-of-way and the overtaking aircraft shall alter course to the right to pass well clear.

Landing. Aircraft on final approach or while landing have the right-of-way over other aircraft in flight or on the ground but shall not take advantage of this rule to force another aircraft off the runway that has already landed and is attempting to clear the runway. When two or more aircraft are approaching to land the aircraft at the lower altitude has the right-of-way, but it should not take advantage of this rule to overtake or cut in front of another aircraft.

FUEL REQUIREMENTS 91.151
Day VFR – Destination plus 30 minutes fuel at normal cruise
Night VFR – Destination plus 45 minutes fuel at normal cruise

AIRSPEED LIMITATIONS 91.117
Below 10,000' MSL	250 KIAS
At or below 2,500' AGL	200 KIAS
Within 4 NM of Class C or Class D airport	
Underneath Class B Airspace or in a VFR corridor (or as noted on chart)	200 KIAS

MINIMUM SAFE ALTITUDES 91.119
Congested Areas – 1,000' above the highest obstacle within 2,000' radius of the aircraft
Sparsely populated – 500' above the surface or no closer than 500' to any person, vehicle, vessel or structure
Anywhere – an altitude that allows an emergency landing without undue hazard to people or property on the ground in the event of a power failure

ATC LIGHT SIGNALS 91.125
•Steady Green:
Ground	Clear to Takeoff
Flight	Clear to Land

•Flashing Green:
Ground	Clear to Taxi
Flight	Return for Landing (to be followed by a Steady Green)

•Steady Red:
Ground	Stop
Flight	Give Way to other Aircraft and Continue Circling

•Flashing Red:
Ground	Taxi Clear of Runway
Flight	Airport Unsafe - Do not Land

•Flashing White:
Ground	Return to Starting Point
Flight	Not Applicable

•Alternating Red & Green:
General Warning - Use Extreme Caution

AIRPORT BEACONS (AIM 2-1-8)
Alternating White and Green Flashes - Lighted Land Airport
Green Alone - Lighted Land Airport with nearby White and Green
Alternating 2 White and 1 Green Flashes - Military Land Airport
Alternating White and Yellow Flashes - Lighted Water Airport
Yellow Alone - Lighted Water Airport with nearby White & Yellow
Alternating Green, Yellow and White - Lighted Heliport

AIRPORTS IN CLASS G AIRSPACE 91.126
Make all turns to the left unless otherwise indicated.
Establish two-way communications prior to reaching 4 NM up to and including 2,500' AGL of airport with operating control tower.
Turbo-jet powered airplanes use the minimum certificated final flap setting as required for conditions and safety.

AIRPORTS IN CLASS E AIRSPACE 91.127
Establish two-way communications prior to reaching 4 NM up to and including 2,500' AGL of airports with operating control towers.
Comply with any traffic patterns established for the airport listed in FAR 93.
ATC clearance/flight plan required for IFR operations.

CLASS D AIRSPACE 91.129
Establish two-way communications prior to entering the airspace.
IFR approaches circle to the left unless otherwise required by ATC.
Large or turbine-powered airplanes fly 1,500' AGL traffic pattern.
Large or turbine-powered airplanes fly at or above the glide slope on approach to ILS equipped runways.
Large or turbine-powered airplanes fly at or above the VASI until lower altitude is necessary for a safe landing.

CLASS C AIRSPACE 91.130
Operational transponder with Mode C.
Establish two-way communications before entering the airspace.
Maintain communications while in Class C airspace.

CLASS B AIRSPACE 91.131
Receive an ATC clearance.
Large turbine aircraft operating to or from the primary airport must remain at or above the floor of Class B airspace.
Student, Recreational and Sport pilots must have required flight and ground instruction and logbook endorsements.
Private pilot certificate required for airports listed in Appendix D.
Must have a VOR or TACAN for IFR flights
Operational transponder with Mode C.
Two-way radio communication capabilities.

RESTRICTED AND PROHIBITED AREAS 91.133
Must receive permission to operate in restricted or prohibited areas by the controlling agency.

CLASS A AIRSPACE 91.135
Instrument Flight Rules.
Clearance and two-way communications required.
Operational transponder with Mode C. If transponder fails ATC may authorize flight to continue.

(30)

VFR WEATHER MINIMUMS 91.155

Airspace	Requirements	Visibility	Cloud Distance
Class A	IFR	N/A	N/A
Class B	Clearance	3 SM	Clear of Clouds
Class C	Communication	3 SM	500/1,000/2,000
Class D	Communication	3 SM	500/1,000/2,000 1,000' Ceiling
Class E	None	3 SM	500/1,000/2,000
Class E & G >10,000 MSL	None	5 SM	1,000/1,000/1 SM
Class G above 1,200' AGL	None	1 SM Day 3 SM Night	Day and Night 500/1,000/2,000
Class G below 1,200 AGL	None	1 SM Day 3 SM Night	Clear of Clouds Day 5,000/1,000/2,000 Night

VFR CRUISING ALTITUDES ABOVE 3,000' AGL 91.159
East 0° to 179°:   Odd Thousands plus 500', 3,500', 5,500' etc
West 180° to 359°: Even Thousands plus 500', 4,500', 6,500' etc

INSTRUMENTS REQUIRED FOR VFR DAY 91.205
Fuel quantity gauge, oil pressure gauge, oil temperature gauge, emergency locator transmitter, altimeter, compass, airspeed indicator, tachometer, manifold pressure gauge (controllable pitch propeller), landing gear position indicator, anti-collision lights for aircraft made after 3/11/1996.

INSTRUMENTS REQUIRED FOR VFR NIGHT 91.205
Anti-collision light system, position lights, electrical generator, spare fuses one complete set or 3 of each kind.

EMERGENCY LOCATOR TRANSMITTER 91.207
Transmits on 121.5 MHz
Not required on training flights within a 50 mile radius.
Battery replaced every 2 years or after 1 hour use.
Operational check every 12 months.

AIRCRAFT LIGHTS 91.209
Between Sunset and Sunrise:
Position Lights - before starting engine and taxiing.
Anti-collision Lights - in-flight.

OXYGEN REQUIREMENTS 91.211
Up to including 12,500' MSL - No Supplemental Oxygen Required
12,501' to 14,000' MSL - Minimum Flight Crew after 30 minutes
14,000' to 15,000' MSL - Minimum Flight Crew entire time
Above 15,000'MSL - All Occupants must be supplied with Oxygen
Supplemental Oxygen recommended above 8,000' MSL at Night

INOPERATIVE EQUIPMENT 91.213
No person may take off an aircraft unless the inoperative equipment is deactivated and marked "inoperative" and it is not part of the minimum equipment required for day or night VFR or IFR flight, as applicable.

TRANSPONDER AND MODE C REQUIRED 91.215
Above 10,000' MSL.
Within Class A, B, and C airspace.
Within 30 nautical radius of Class B primary airport.
Over flying Class B or Class C airspace.
Transponder and Mode C on in controlled airspace.

AEROBATIC FLIGHT 91.303
Not allowed over a congested area, an open assembly of persons, Class B, C, D airspace or Class E airspace designated for an airport, within a federal airway, below 1,500' AGL, with less than 3 miles visibility.

USE OF PARACHUTES 91.307(c)
Parachutes are required for maneuver exceeding 60° bank or 30° pitch unless training required for a certificate or rating.

COMMUNICATIONS FAILURE PROCEDURES
Squawk 7600 on the transponder.
Stay clear until the direction of traffic in the pattern can be determined.
Tune receiver or transmit on the tower frequency as able.
Flash your landing light or wave your wings when able to acknowledge transmissions or light signals.

NTSB 830
Immediate notification to the National Transportation Safety Board is required for the following:
(1) An aircraft accident involving serious injury or death or substantial aircraft damage.
(2) Flight control system failure or malfunction.
(3) Inability of a required crewmember to perform normal flight duties as a result of injury or illness.
(4) Turbine engine structural component failure excluding compressor or turbine blades or vanes.
(5) In-flight fire.
(6) Aircraft collide in-flight.
(7) Property damage in excess of $25,000.00.
(8) An aircraft overdue believed to be involved in an accident.

(32)

NTSB 830 CONTINUED
For large multiengine aircraft more than 12,500 pounds:
(9) Electrical system failure requiring sustained use of emergency bus from back up source for to retain flight control or essential instruments.
(10) In-flight hydraulic system failure resulting use of sole remaining system or mechanical backup for operation of flight controls.
(11) Sustained loss of power or thrust by two or more engines.
(12) Evacuation of an aircraft using the emergency egress system.

FAR PART 43 PREVENTATIVE MAINTANENCE
Under FAR Part 43 a pilot may perform the following preventative maintenance on the aircraft he owns or operates:
Remove and replace landing gear tires.
Service landing gear struts with air and fluid.
Service wheel bearings, cleaning and greasing.
Lubrication requiring only normal removal of cowls, covers and fairings.
Making simple fabric patches not requiring rib stitching or removal of control surfaces or structural parts.
Replenish hydraulic fluid reservoirs.
Make small simple repairs to fairings, covers, cowls and small patches and reinforcements not changing contour to change proper air-flow.
Replace safety belts.
Replace seats or seat parts approved for aircraft.
Trouble-shoot and repair broken wires in landing light circuit.
Replace bulbs and lenses of position and landing lights.
Replacing wheels and skis where no weight and balance computation is required.
Replace, clean and gap spark plugs.
Replace hose connection except hydraulic hoses.
Clean fuel and oil filters and screens.
Replace batteries. Check battery fluid level and specific gravity.
Additional maintenance must be performed under the direct supervision of a certified aircraft mechanic.

NASA AVIATION SAFETY REPORTING SYSTEM
ASRS reports are confidential and will prevent civil penalty or certificate suspension if: (1) The violation was inadvertent, not deliberate. (2) The violation did not involve a criminal offense, accident, or lack of competence. (3) The pilot did not commit another violation since filing the report. (4) The ASRS report is filed within 10 days. NASA ARC Form 277 may be obtained at a FSS, FSDO, or write to: FAA Aeronautical Center, Distribution Section, AAC-45C, P.O. Box 189, Moffett Field, CA 94035 or at: www.asrs.arc.nasa.gov/forms.htm

INSTRUMENT FLIGHT RULES

IFR RECENT EXPERIENCE 61.57
6 Months: Within the preceding 6 calendar months.
6 Approaches: All 6 may be done in a simulator.
Holding Procedures
Intercepting and Tracking Courses

IFR DEPARTURES
Instrument Departure Procedures are established where obstacles penetrate a climb plane of 152'/NM beginning at 35' above the departure end of the runway. Unless otherwise stated a 200'/NM climb rate is required to provide a minimum clearance of 48' per NM.

CIVIL AIRPORT TAKEOFF MINIMUMS
1 mile visibility for 1 or 2 engine aircraft and $\frac{1}{2}$ mile for 3 or more engine aircraft. Minimum ceiling, visibility and climb rates are noted for particular runways where additional obstacle clearance is required.

CLEARANCE VOID TIME
Issued by ATC when departing into uncontrolled airspace. ATC must be informed within 30 minutes if the flight did not depart.

VOR ACCURACY CHECK
Required for IFR flight within the past 30 days recording: date, place, bearing error and signature.
Ground Check   ± 4°
VOT Test Signal   ± 4°
Dual VOR Check   within 4°
Airborne Check   ±6°

IFR FLIGHT FUEL REQUIREMENTS 91.167
An IFR flight must have enough fuel to fly to the destination, alternate and then for 45 minutes more based on the weather reports and forecasts.

ALTERNATE AIRPORT NOT REQUIRED 91.169
When destination airport weather is forecast ± 1 hour of ETA greater than 2,000'ceiling and 3 miles visibility

ALTERNATE AIRPORT WEATHER MINIMUMS 91.169
Weather forecasts at the ETA must be 600' ceiling and 2 miles visibility for airports with a precision approach, 800' ceiling and 2 miles visibility for airports with a non-precision approach.

(34)

IFR ALTITUDES

MEA Minimum Enroute Altitude - navigation reception, obstacle clearance (1,000' within 4 NM, 2,000' in mountainous areas)

MOCA Minimum Obstruction Clearance Altitude - navigation reception and obstacle clearance only within 22 miles of the VOR

MCA Minimum Crossing Altitude - obstacle clearance with normal climb

MRA Minimum Reception Altitude navigation reception of the intersection, obstacle clearance

MSA Minimum Sector Altitude - 1,000' obstacle clearance within 25 miles of navaid

MAA Maximum Authorized Altitude - below Special Use Airspace

MVA Minimum Vectoring Altitude - at least 500' obstacle clearance during radar vectors

IFR CRUISING ALTITUDES AND FLIGHT LEVELS: 91.179

East 0° to 179°:   Odd Thousands, 3,000' MSL, 5,000' MSL, etc
West 180° to 359°: Even Thousands, 4,000' MSL, 6,000' MSL, etc

FLIGHT LEVELS FROM FL 180 TO FL 290

East 0° to 179°:   Odd Flight Levels, FL 190, FL 210, FL230,
West 180° to 359°: Even Flight Levels, FL 180, FL 200, etc

RVSM FLIGHT LEVELS FROM FL 290 TO FL 410 AT 2,000' INTERVALS

East 0° to 179°:   Odd Flight Levels, FL 290, FL310, to FL 410
West 180° to 359°: Even Flight Levels, FL 300, FL320 to FL 400

NON-RVSM FLIGHT LEVELS FROM FL 430 TO FL 600 AT 4,000' INTERVALS

East 0° to 179°:   Flight Levels, FL 450, FL 490, FL530 etc
West 180° to 359°: Flight Levels, FL 430, FL 470, FL 510 , etc

POSITION REPORTS (AIM 5-3-2)

Identification.
Position.
Time.
Altitude.
Type of flight plan (FSS only).
ETA and name of next reporting fix.
Name of succeeding reporting point.
Remarks.

INSTRUMENTS REQUIRED FOR IFR 91.205

Clock with seconds, directional gyro, attitude indicator, rate of turn indicator, two-way radio and navigational equipment appropriate to the ground facilities being used, DME above FL 240 when VOR navigation is being used, generator, adjustable altimeter and a slip-skid indicator.

REQUIRED IFR COMMUNICATIONS TO ATC WITHOUT SPECIFIC REQUEST

At All Times:
Any unforecast weather conditions. (FAR 91.183)
Anything affecting the safety of the flight. (FAR 91.183)
Loss or impairment of communication or navigational equipment and degree of assistance desired from ATC (FAR 91.187, AIM 5-3-3).
Missed approach and intentions. (AIM 5-3-3)
Vacating an assigned altitude. (AIM 5-3-3)
Change in altitude while VFR-On-Top. (AIM 5-3-3)
Unable to climb or descend 500 fpm. (AIM 5-3-3)
Change in TAS of 10 knots or 5% (greater of). (AIM 5-3-3)
Time and altitude reaching a clearance limit or holding fix. (AIM 5-3-3, AIM 5-3-7)
Leaving an assigned holding fix. (AIM 5-3-3, 5-3-7)

When Not in Radar Contact:
Time and altitude passing a designated reporting point. (FAR 91.183, AIM 5-3-2)
Over reporting points used to define a direct route. (AIM 5-3-2)
Final approach fix or outer marker inbound. (AIM 5-3-3)
Change in ETA to next reporting point in excess of ±3 minutes. (AIM 5-3-3)

LOSS OF COMMUNICATIONS FAR 91.185
Route to Fly (AVE. F):
    A - Assigned
    V - Vectored
    E - Expected
    F - Filed
Altitude, highest of for the route segment being flown (MEA):
    M - Minimum IFR Altitude
    E - Expected as Advised by ATC
    A - Assigned by ATC
Leave Holding Fix:
    To arrive at the IAF but not before:
    Expected approach clearance time
    ETA on flight plan
Descent for Approach:
    From enroute altitude upon reaching the IAF but not before:
    Expected approach clearance time
    ETA on flight plan

ATC CLEARANCE ITEMS

Clearance Limit: The airport or a fix to which the flight is cleared.

Departure Procedure: Headings to fly, altitude restrictions. SID's when used, and an initial departure fix.

Route of Flight: The route requested by the pilot or a preferred routing assigned by ATC.

Altitude Data: The altitude filed by the pilot to be maintained or a block of airspace when assigned a CRUISE clearance.

Holding Instructions: The fix to hold at when a delay is expected.

Frequency & Squawk The frequency on which to contact Departure Control and your discreet transponder code assignment.

VFR-ON-TOP CLEARANCE (AIM 4-4-7)

Both VFR and IFR rules apply. Maintain appropriate VFR altitudes, cloud clearances and visibility minimums. Report changes in altitude to ATC. Separation is not always provided. Pilot is responsible to see-and-avoid other aircraft.

IFR CLIMB TO VFR-ON-TOP CONDITIONS (AIM 4-4-7)

IFR flight plan. May include a clearance limit. Say direction of flight or destination. Clearance will contain a top report if available. Report reaching VFR-On-Top. If not VFR-On-Top at a specified altitude advise ATC.

CRUISE CLEARANCE (AIM 4-4-3)

Assigns block of airspace. Pilot may climb and descend between the MEA and assigned altitude. Once verbally reporting a descent from an altitude in the block, the pilot may not longer return to that altitude.

CONTACT APPROACH (AIM 5-4-22)

Only on request, not assigned by ATC. Airport must have an IAP, 1 mile visibility, clear of clouds and reasonably expect to continue to the airport. Separation provided between IFR and SVFR traffic.

VISUAL APPROACH (AIM 5-4-20)

Still on an IFR flight plan. VFR minimums apply. Must have airport or preceding aircraft in sight. No missed approach procedure.

HOLDING INSTRUCTIONS (AIM 5-3-7)

Holding fix
Direction from the fix
Radial, course, bearing or airway to hold on
Leg length for DME/RNAV, or leg time in minutes
Left turns if required
EFC time

HOLDING AIRSPEED LIMITATIONS (AIM 5-3-7)
MHA through 6,000' MSL   - 200 KIAS
6,001' through 14,000' MSL   - 230 KIAS
Above 14,000' MSL   - 265 KIAS
A maximum airspeed other than standard may be depicted either
inside or next to the charted racetrack symbol.

LOCALIZER
4° to 6° wide, usually 5°. 4 times more sensitive than a VOR. 1 dot
on the localizer equals about 1/2°or about 50' per dot per NM. 1
dot at the MM λ 100', at the OM λ 300'. Antennas at the far end
of the runway produce a signal 700' wide at the threshold. When
flying inbound on back course or outbound on front course, fly
away from the needle. HSI tuned to the front course will always
indicate normal sensing.

GLIDE SLOPE
1.4° full scale. 1 dot on the glide slope ≈ 1/10° or about 10' per NM
per dot. 1 dot at the MM λ 8', at the OM λ 50'. The antenna is
located 1,000' from the threshold abeam the fixed distance
marker. GS indications are unusable from 18 to 27 above
touchdown and would theoretically would bring the aircraft to
touchdown at the fixed distance marker. Normally a 3° glide angle.
GS angle coincides with VASI. Intercepting GS from below is safe
to avoid "false" signal. Crosscheck intercept altitude at FAF.

MARKER BEACONS
Broadcast at 75 MHz. Set sensitivity to low for greater accuracy
at MM, set to high for suspicious signal or earlier warning at MM.

OUTER MARKER (OM)
Blue, 120 dashes per minute. May be substituted by compass
locator, charted VOR/NDB fix, DME or radar. Located 4 to 7 NM
from runway. Glide slope crosses OM typically at λ 1,500' HAT.

LOCATOR OUTER MARKERS (LOM)
25 watt transmitters with a range of 15 miles. LOM identifier will
be the first two letters of the localizer after the "I".

MIDDLE MARKER (MM)
Amber, 95 dots and dashes per minute. Located 0.4 to 0.6 usually
0.5 NM from runway threshold. The MM will be received at or just
after reaching decision altitude. A 200' decision height is raised
50' without MM. A 250' DH would not be raised without MM. A
visual of the runway threshold from the MM will meet the in-
flight visibility minimums. Substitution for the MM would be a
Locator Middle Marker or precision radar. Locator Middle Marker
(LMM), will broadcast the last two letters of the associated
localizer.

(38)

INNER MARKER
White, 360 dots per minute. Located between the MM and the landing threshold used for CAT-2 approaches with a 100' DH.

BACK COURSE MARKERS
White, pairs of audio dots, used on back course approaches

FAN MARKER
White, dot-dash-dot or dash-dot-dash signal. Used for along airway and non-precision approach fixes.

ALSF-1 AND ALSF-2
Approach Lighting System with Sequence Flashing Lights are large systems installed at Category I and II runways and are the only systems which have the red terminating and side row bars respectively, which allow descent below 100' HAT when in view.

SALS/SALSF
Short Approach Lighting System/with Sequenced Flashing Lights are 1,500' long and are the same as the inner 1,500' of the ALSF-1. The light bars are 100' apart.

SSALR/SSALF
Simplified Short Approach Lighting System have the same basic configuration of 1,400' long with the light bars spaced 200'apart.

MALSR/MALSF
Medium Intensity Approach Lighting System have the same basic configuration of 1,400' long with the light bars spaced 200'apart.

SSALR/MALSR
RAIL extends the ALS to 2,400' to 3,000' for use with precision instrument approach runways.

SSALF/MALSF
1,400' long with the Sequenced Flashing Lights spaced in between the light bars. Usually for non-precision instrument approach runways.

DECISION/HORIZON BAR
Located 1,000' from the runway threshold on all Approach Lighting Systems. If you can just see the decision bar at the MM subtract 1,000' from your MM distance to the runway to estimate the in-flight visibility.

RUNWAY ALIGNMENT INDICATOR LIGHTS (RAIL) & SEQUENCED FLASHING LIGHTS (F)

The "rabbit", produce the illusion of a ball of light traveling toward the threshold. The RAIL extends beyond the ALS increasing its length from 1,400' to 2,400' or 3,000'. Sequenced Flashing Lights are placed in between the light bars and do not extend past the ALS.

RUNWAY END IDENTIFIER LIGHTS (REIL)

Flashing lights on each side of the runway threshold for quick identification of the runway.

RUNWAY VISUAL RANGE

RVR minimums are converted to ground visibility when the RVR is inoperative. The ground visibility will then be the visibility minimum for takeoff or landing on that runway.

1600 RVR	1/4 statute mile
2400 RVR	1/2 statute mile
3200 RVR	5/8 statute mile
4000 RVR	3/4 statute mile
4500 RVR	7/8 statute mile
5000 RVR	1 statute mile
6000 RVR	1 1/4 statute mile

PILOT CONTROLLED LIGHTING

Keying the mike will turn on the ALS and runway lights. 7 times for high, 5 times for medium, 3 times for low. The REIL may be turned off at some airports when keying 5 or 3 times. The lights will stay on for 15 minutes.

DESCENT BELOW DECISION HEIGHT OR MDA

The aircraft must be continuously in a position from which a normal descent to landing with normal maneuvers can be made. Part 121 and 135 require the descent allows touchdown within the touchdown zone of the runway. Flight visibility may not be less than the minimum visibility required for the approach. At least one of the following visual references is distinctly visible and identifiable to the pilot:

• Threshold, Threshold Lights, Threshold markings.
• Runway End Identifier Lights. (REIL)
• Visual Approach Slope Indicator (VASI).
• Touchdown Zone (TDZ).
• Touchdown Zone Markings or Lights (TDZL).
• Runway, Runway Markings or Runway Lights.
• Approach Light System – Not to descend below 100 feet above the touchdown zone unless the red terminating or siderow bars (ALSF1/2) or the runway environment is in sight.

AIRCRAFT APPROACH CATEGORIES/CIRCLING RADII
AIM 5-4-7, 5-4-18

CAT A	91 knots or less	1.3 miles
CAT B	91 to 120 knots	1.5 miles
CAT C	121 to 140 knots	1.7 miles
CAT D	141 to 165 knots	2.3 miles
CAT E	166 knots or greater	4.5 miles

MISSED APPROACH FAR 91.175
A missed approach procedure must be flown when below MDA, at MAP or DH and the landing requirements are not met or when circling to land at or above the MDA and an identifiable part of the airport is not distinctly visible (unless vision is blocked from normal aircraft banking).

MISSED APPROACH SEGMENT
Climb straight ahead or climbing turn.
Turn toward the airport if circling to land.
Continue to the MAP before turning.
Missed Approach Point is determined by groundspeed/time, DME or navaid station passage. The missed approach segment provides obstacle clearance in a 40:1 plane (152'/NM) from the Missed Approach Point. Obstacle clearance may be no greater than provided at the MAP.

CIRCLE TO LAND
Keep the runway in sight, stay at MDA. Take the shortest route to base or downwind of landing runway. Use left traffic when possible for better visibility. Make a climbing turn toward airport for a missed approach.

PROCEDURE TURNS
Procedure Turns are charted when the difference between the terminal route and the final approach segment is more than 30° or the FAF altitude is more than 300' lower than the terminal route altitude. Any type of course reversal is allowed on the protected side. Holding pattern procedure turns may be entered from any direction but must be flown as charted. Procedure turns are the initial approach segment beginning at the IAF and provide 1,000' obstacle clearance. Once established inbound begins the intermediate segment and 500' clearance is provided.
Procedure Turn Holding Patterns are charted when there is not enough space for a standard procedure turn.
NoPT means a procedure turn is not required or authorized unless cleared with ATC. A procedure turn is required when charted unless NoPT is printed on the route.

INITIAL APPROACH FIX (IAF)
Approach begins, initial approach segment, at IAF.

INITIAL APPROACH SEGMENT

DME arc, radial, course, heading radar vector or combination, 1,000' obstacle clearance, maximum descent gradient 500'/NM. Purpose; to align the aircraft with the intermediate segment. Procedure turn outbound is always the Initial approach segment altitude.

INTERMEDIATE APPROACH SEGMENT

Designed to reduce pilot work load and configure for FAS. Begins at fix 5 to 15 NM (localizer minimum 1 NM depending on intercept angle) before the FAF and is not marked on chart. Ends at FAF. 500' obstacle clearance and maximum descent angle of 300'/NM, optimum 150'/NM, within 30° of FAC. Example: outbound procedure turn – initial approach segment, inbound procedure turn – intermediate approach segment. Approaches without FAF do not have an intermediate approach segment.

FINAL APPROACH SEGMENT

Final Approach Segment begins at FAF. Obstacle clearance on an ILS approach at DH is variable. Straight in VOR may be only 250' clearance at MDA. Circling may be only 300'.

FINAL APPROACH FIX (FAF)

Maltese cross is indicated whenever timing is required. No FAF is established when the VOR or NDB is located on the airport within 1 NM of the landing runway.

MISSED APPROACH POINT (MAP)

Established by timing, DME, marker beacon or station passage. VOR cross-fixes are not used because of workload on pilot and low reception altitude.

FAR PART 135

APPLICABILITY 135.1
Part 135 rules apply to air taxi operations, aircraft carrying US mail under contract, air commerce operations with aircraft having a seating capacity of less than 20 passenger seats or a maximum payload of less than 6,000 pounds.

LOAD MANIFEST 135.63(c)
For multiengine aircraft the manifest must include: number of passengers, takeoff weight, maximum allowable takeoff weight for that flight (performance, maximum landing weight considered), center of gravity limits (for takeoff and landing), center of gravity (at takeoff and landing), registration number, origin and destination, names of crewmembers. Manifest must be on board the aircraft and copies kept at the base for 30 days.

AIRCRAFT MAINTENANCE LOG 135.65
Each aircraft shall have a maintenance log on board that the pilot in command can review the status of deferred or corrected items before each flight.

PILOT USE OF OXYGEN 135.89
10,000' to 12,000' for more than 30 minutes. Above 12,000' at all times. Above 25,000' if one pilot leaves the flight deck the other pilot shall wear and use an oxygen mask, (unless quick-donning type). Above 35,000' one pilot shall wear and use an oxygen mask.

PASSENGER USE OF OXYGEN 135.157
10,000' to 15,000' oxygen must be supplied to 10% of the passengers for flights more than 30 minutes. Above 15,000' each occupant must be supplied with oxygen. Above 25,000' a 10 minute supply of oxygen to each occupant for use during emergency descent.

EXTENDED OVERWATER OPERATIONS 1.1
A horizontal distance of more than 50 miles from the shoreline.

EMERGENCY EQUIPMENT, EXTENDED OVERWATER OPERATIONS 135.167
Each passenger must have an approved life vest. Approved life rafts with enough capacity for the occupants of the aircraft.

AUTOPILOT USE MINIMUM ALTITUDES 135.93
While enroute no less than 500'AGL or no less than twice the maximum altitude loss whichever is greater. On approach no less than 50 below the minimum descent altitude or less than twice the maximum altitude loss in approach mode whichever is greater.

(43)

SECOND IN COMMAND REQUIRED 135.101
Two pilots are required for flight carrying passengers under Instrument Flight Rules.

AUTOPILOT IN LIEU OF SECOND IN COMMAND 135.105
A pilot with at least 100 hours as pilot in command in the make and model may be approved to use a 3 axis autopilot in lieu of a second in command.

PASSENGER BRIEFING 135.117
Smoking, use of seatbelts, placement of seat backs, location and operation of emergency exits, location of survival equipment, ditching procedures and use of floatation equipment, location and use of fire extinguishers, briefing cards.

ALCOHOLIC BEVERAGES 135.121
No operator may serve an intoxicated person. No operator may not allow an intoxicated person to board the aircraft. The operator must serve any drinks consumed on the aircraft.

COCKPIT VOICE RECORDERS 135.151
CVR's are required on multiengine, turbine or rotorcraft with 6 or more passenger seats requiring 2 pilots and operated from the beginning of the first checklist to the end of the last checklist.

GROUND PROXIMITY WARNING SYSTEM 135.153
GPWS are required on turbine powered aircraft with 10 or more passenger seats.

FIRE EXTINGUISHERS 135.155
One hand fire extinguisher must be available in the flight deck and one available in the passenger compartment.

INSTRUMENTS REQUIRED FOR VFR NIGHT 135.159
Rate of turn, slip/skid, attitude indicator, heading indicator, generator, flashlight with 2 D cells, adequate instrument lighting

INSTRUMENTS REQUIRED FOR IFR FLIGHT 135.163
Vertical speed indicator, OAT gauge, heated pitot, vacuum/power failure warning indicator for gyros, alternate static source.

INOPERABLE INSTRUMENTS AND EQUIPMENT 135.179
An approved Minimum Equipment List is required to operate an aircraft with inoperable instruments or equipment.

TRAFFIC ALERT & COLLISION AVOIDANCE SYSTEM 135.180
TCAS is required on turbine powered aircraft with 10 or more passenger seats.

PERFORMANCE REQUIRED IFR OR OVER THE TOP CONDITIONS 135.181
Multiengine aircraft must be able to climb 50 fpm above 5,000'MSL with the critical engine inoperative or descent under VFR. Single engine aircraft must be able to descent under VFR if the engine fails.

LAND AIRCRAFT OVER WATER 135.183
Single engine aircraft must be able to reach land in the engine fails, multiengine aircraft must be able to climb 50 fpm at 1,000' MSL with critical engine inoperative.

EMPTY WEIGHT AND CENTER OF GRAVITY 135.185
Multiengine aircraft must be weighed every 36 calendar months.

VFR MINIMUM ALTITUDES 135.203
Daytime no less than 500' above the surface and 500' horizontal distance from any obstacle. At night no less than 1,000' above the highest obstacle within 5 miles. Designated mountainous terrain 2,000' above the highest obstacle within 5 miles.

VFR VISIBILITY REQUIRMENTS 135.205
Uncontrolled airspace minimum ceiling is 1,000' and visibility is 2 statute miles

IFR TAKEOFF LIMITATIONS 135.219
If the weather is above takeoff minimums but below landing minimums, an alternate airport is required within 1 hour flight time in still air.

CIVIL AIRPORT TAKEOFF MINIMUMS 91.175
1 statute miles visibility for 1 or 2 engine aircraft, 1/2 statute miles visibility for 3 or more engine aircraft.

LOWER TAKEOFF MINIMUMS (WHEN AUTHORIZED)
1600 TDZRVR or 1/4 mile visibility with: HIRL, CL, RCLM or adequate visual reference. Mid RVR may be substituted if TDZRVR not available.
1200 TDRVR and 1000 RORVR with: Operative CL. Mid RVR may substitute for TDZRVR or RORVR.
500 TDZRVR, 500 MDRVR and 500 RORVR with: CL and RCLM. Any one RVR report may be missing if remaining two are above minimums. 2 pilots are required with 2 independent sets of flight instruments. The PIC must have at least 100 hours as PIC in make and model, the SIC must have 100 hours in make and model. Both pilots must have completed the company's approved training program for these takeoffs.

(45)

ALTERNATE AIRPORT WEATHER MINIMUMS PART 135.221
To use an airport as an alternate the weather must be forecast to be at or above the authorized alternate airport minimums at the estimated time of arrival (at the alternate)

ALTERNATE AIRPORT REQUIREMENTS PART 135.223
1-2-3 Rule for Destination Airport
1 hour before and one hour after the estimated time of arrival:
2,000' ceiling or 1,500' above circling MDA or lowest MDA (no circling authorized) whichever is higher
3 miles visibility or 2 miles more than the minimum visibility for the approach to be used whichever is greater

IFR TAKEOFF APPROACH & LANDING MINIMUMS 135.225
A pilot may not begin an instrument approach unless the weather is reported at or above the landing minimums. If the weather goes below landing minimum inside the FAF or established procedure turn inbound on approaches without a FAF, the approach may be continued. Pilots of turbine-powered aircraft without 100 hours PIC in type will increase landing minimums by 100' and 1/2 mile.

VFR FUEL SUPPLY 135.209
Day: destination plus 30 minutes
Night: destination plus 45 minutes

FLIGHT TIME LIMITATIONS UNSCHEDULED ONE AND TWO CREW OPERATIONS 135.267
500 hours in a calendar quarter, 800 hours in 2 consecutive quarters, 1,400 hours in a calendar year. Maximum of 8 hours for single pilots, 10 hours for 2 crew pilots within a 14 hour assigned duty period during 24 consecutive hours followed by 10 hours consecutive rest. If the flight time is exceeded:

Exceeded flight time	Rest required
30 minutes	11 hours rest
30 to 60 minutes	12 hours rest
60 minutes or more	16 hours rest

13 rest periods of at least 24 hours are required in a calendar quarter.
Positioning flight to a 135 flight counts as flight and duty time. Positioning after a 135 flight counts as duty time but not as flight time (daily limitations).

EMERGENCIES

IN-FLIGHT ENGINE POWER FAILURE
Fly at Best Glide Airspeed
Select Suitable Landing Area
Check for Carburetor Icing
Check Fuel Selector, Try Switching Tanks
Check Fuel Primer In and Locked
Check Magnetos On Both, Try Left or Right Magneto
Transmit Position and Situation to ATC

TWIN ENGINE AIRCRAFT SINGLE ENGINE FAILURE
Maintain Heading
Maintain V_{YSE}
Mixture, Props, Throttles Forward
Identify - Dead Foot Dead Engine
Verify - Retard Throttle of Suspected Failed Engine
Troubleshoot Affected Engine
Feather as Required

EMERGENCY COMMUNICATIONS
Squawk 7700
Transmit "Mayday, Mayday, Mayday"
Name of Station you are calling
Aircraft Type and Identification
Nature of Emergency
Position, Heading and Altitude
Fuel Remaining
Number of Persons on Board
Weather Conditions
Intentions or Assistance Desired

ELECTRICAL FIRE
Master Switch Off
Locate source and extinguish
Pull circuit breaker to isolate affected equipment
Carefully turn master switch on
Ventilate cabin
Land as soon as practicable

ENGINE FIRE
Mixture control off.
Fuel valve shutoff
Retard throttle
Do not restart engine
Slideslip if necessary to keep flame away from cabin
Land immediately

(47)

HYPOXIA - Lack of sufficient oxygen
Symptoms: sense of well being or belligerence, fatigue, impaired thinking, headache, fingernails and lips turn blue color
Heavy smokers may show symptoms earlier than non-smokers.
Night vision may be impaired above 8,000' MSL
Treatment - descend immediately, open windows, turn off cabin heater, use supplemental oxygen if available

CARBON MONOXIDE POISONING - Breathing leaking exhaust fumes reduces the blood's ability to carry oxygen.
Symptoms - similar to hypoxia, undue fatigue, impaired thinking, dizziness, dull headache
Treatment -Open windows, turn off cabin heat

HYPERVENTILATION - Blowing off excessive carbon dioxide
Symptoms - similar to hypoxia, lightheadedness, suffocation, tingling in the extremities, coolness, rapid breathing
Treatment - Slow breathing, breath in a paper bag, if using oxygen set to 100%

DECOMPRESSION SICKNESS AFTER SCUBA DIVING
For cabin altitudes of 8,000' or less wait at least 12 hours after a dive, 24 hours after a dive that required a controlled ascent
For cabin altitudes above 8,000' wait 24 hours after any dive.

EMERGENCY RESUSCITATION
Lay victim on back and clear mouth of mucus and foreign objects
Raise neck with one hand and tilt head as far back as possible
Close victims nostrils with fingers and place mouth over victims mouth. Exhale into victims mouth. Watch victims chest expand.
Give four quick full breaths. If airway is blocked try abdominal or chest thrusts. Clear airway with finger probes.
Check for pulse on sides of neck. If no pulse is present place heel of one hand on lower half of breastbone and cover with other hand. Press down firmly and quickly 1 1/2 to 2 inches and release.
One rescuer: Inflate lungs twice and compress heart 15 times, once per second. Two rescuers: Inflate lungs every 5th heart compression.

SURVIVAL ON LAND
Stay clear of airplane until fuel has evaporated. Caution for electrical sparks.
Check injuries and give first aid. Use caution moving injured people with possible neck or back injuries.
Get out of wind and rain. Find or construct shelter. Start a fire if necessary. Rest until you are over the shock of the crash.
Have signaling equipment ready. Make sure ELT is transmitting.
Stay near aircraft. Organize camp. Look for water supply.
Prepare signals so you can be seen from the air.

SURVIVAL KIT ITEMS
First Aid - Band-Aids, medical adhesive tape, triangular bandages, aspirin, antiseptic ointment, razor knife, first aid book
Food - drinking water, water purification tablets, meals ready to eat (MRE surplus), candy bars, fruit bars, dehydrated soups, coffee and milk, sugar, salt, tea, hard candy, gum, heavy duty aluminum foil to be used for cooking and utensils.
Tools - personal strobe lights, chemical lights, survival knife, whistle, waterproof matches, metal match, lighter, safety pins, space blankets, fishing line, hooks, wire for snares, signal mirror, compass, flashlight with batteries stored separately, aluminum cooking pot, plastic garbage bags, survival book.

COLD WEATHER SURVIVAL
Protection from cold is the most immediate problem. Check for frostbite. Immediately warm area of possible frostbite with body heat or warm water. Keep clothing dry. Avoid overexertion and sweating in heavy clothes. Work slowly. Construct a shelter and line with branches to stay dry and warm. Aluminum aircraft fuselages conduct heat away rapidly and do not make good shelters. Interior fabric and insulation can be salvaged. Collect wood, fuel, oil, brush and sticks to build a fire.

DESERT
Water is the biggest concern. Keep head and neck covered, stay in the shade. A person who does not exert himself can survive 2 to 3 days in temperatures of 100°F or more without water. The aircraft fuselage may be to hot for shelter in the day time, but can offer protection from poisonous snakes at night. Travel if you think you can reach assistance and if you have enough water. Travel only at night. Day time surface temperatures can be reduced by as much as 30° by digging 2 feet below the surface. Temperatures are also 20° cooler one foot above the surface.

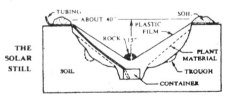

THE SOLAR STILL

A solar still can be constructed as illustrated. Dig a hole 3 feet around and 2 feet deep in the lowest land available. If possible line the hole with moist plant material. Do not let the plastic touch the sides of the pit at any point. Undrinkable water may be purified by pouring in a trough dug inside the hole.

TROPICS
Find shelter from rain sun and insects. Insects are most immediate danger, protect yourself against bites.

SURVIVAL AT SEA
Stay clear fuel saturated water. Salvage floating equipment. Use caution to remain clear of sharp objects that may snag raft. Rig up a windbreak for protection against sun, wind and rain. Conserve food and water by conserving energy and staying calm. Use sea markers during daytime. Rewrap them when not in use.

FOOD
Take stock of available food and water. Conserve your food intake. Eating dry starchy foods and meat increases thirst. Hard candy and fruit bars are the most efficient. Don't nibble on food. Plan one or two meals per day. Traveling requires about twice as much food as staying in place. The more work you do the more food and water you will need. If water is plentiful, drink more than you normally would to keep fit.

HEALTH
Save your strength. Rest 10 minutes each hour while working. Get lots of sleep. Take care of your feet if traveling. If your feet hurt stop and take care of them. Put tape on skin where your shoe are rubbing to avoid blisters. Guard against skin infections. Use antiseptic cream on all cuts, scratches and insect bites. Guard against intestinal sickness. Boil drinking water for 10 minutes and cook all food when possible.

EMERGENCY LOCATOR TRANSMITTER
Place on high ground
Do not turn off at night
Transmits for 2 days

SURVIVAL STATISTICS - Search and Rescue Initiated
IFR	34 minutes
VFR	5 hours 30 minutes
NO VFR FLIGHT PLAN	35 hours

AVERAGE SURVIVAL TIME AFTER A CRASH
Injured persons:	24 hours
Uninjured persons:	72 hours

90% of persons are inadequately dressed for crash site

AVERAGE TIME SURVIVORS FOUND AFTER SEARCH BEGUN
IFR	3 hours
VFR	38 hours
NO VFR FLIGHT PLAN	81 hours

(50)

DITCHING
High winds, rough seas ditch into the wind
Light winds heavy swells ditch parallel to swells, avoid face of swells
Put on life jackets
Jettison heavy baggage
Unlatch doors prior to contact with water
Evacuate aircraft and stay clear of gas saturated water.

SIGNALING
Personal strobe lights can be seen for up to 12 miles at night. Use a signal mirror or punch a hole in the center of a piece of shiny metal and practice signaling. A piece of glass with one side covered with mud or a smooth wet piece of wood can make a usable signal mirror. In haze, the aircraft will see the flash of the signal mirror before the survivors can see the aircraft, so signal in the direction of the sound of the aircraft. Day time use smoke signals. Night time use red flares. Keep signal flares dry and be careful of fire hazard when using signal flares. Fire is the most noticeable signaling tool the survivor has at his disposal. Have signal fires ready to light when search aircraft are heard. Use oils, oil soaked rags, rubber to make black smoke. Green leaves or moss will make white smoke. Night time make bright fire or use flashlights or signal flares. Use sea markers during daytime. Rewrap them when not in use.

GROUND TO AIR CODE FOR SURVIVORS TO AIR RESCUE

NEED MEDICAL ASSISTANCE—URGENT
Used only when life is at stake

ALL OK—DO NOT WAIT
Wave one arm overhead

CAN PROCEED SHORTLY— WAIT IF PRACTICABLE
One arm horizontal

NEED MECHANICAL HELP OR PARTS—LONG DELAY
Both arms horizontal

USE DROP MESSAGE
Make throwing motion

OUR RECEIVER IS OPERATING
Cup hands over ears

DO NOT ATTEMPT TO LAND HERE
Both arms waved across face

LAND HERE
Both arms forward horizontally, squatting and point in direction of landing—Repeat

NEGATIVE (NO)
White cloth waved horizontally

AFFIRMATIVE (YES)
White cloth waved vertically

PICK US UP— PLANE ABANDONED
Both arms vertical

AFFIRMATIVE (YES)
Dip nose of plane several times

NEGATIVE (NO)
Fishtail plane

HOW TO USE THEM

If you are forced down and are able to attract the attention of the pilot of a rescue airplane, the body signals illustrated on this page can be used to transmit messages to him as he circles over your location. Stand in the open when you make the signals. Be sure that the background, as seen from the air, is not confusing. Go through the motions slowly and repeat each signal until you are positive that the pilot understands you.

NO.	MESSAGE	CODE SYMBOL
1	Require assistance	V
2	Require medical assistance	X
3	No or Negative	N
4	Yes or Affirmative	Y
5	Proceeding in this direction	↑

WIND CHILL FACTOR

WIND MPH	OUTSIDE AIR TEMPERATURE FARHENHEIT									
	50	45	40	35	30	25	20	15	10	5
4	50	45	40	35	30	25	20	15	10	5
6	46	41	35	30	24	19	13	8	2	-3
8	43	37	31	25	20	14	8	2	-4	-10
10	40	34	28	22	16	10	4	-3	-9	-15
12	38	32	26	19	13	6	0	-7	-13	-19
14	37	30	23	17	10	3	-3	-10	-17	-23
16	35	28	21	15	8	1	-6	-13	-20	-26
18	34	27	20	13	6	-1	-8	-15	-22	-29
20	32	25	18	11	4	-3	-10	-18	-25	-32
22	31	24	17	10	2	-5	-12	-19	-27	-34
24	30	23	16	8	1	-6	-14	-21	-29	-36
26	30	22	15	7	0	-8	-15	-23	-30	-38
28	29	21	14	6	-1	-9	-17	-24	-32	-39
30	28	21	13	5	-2	-10	-18	-25	-33	-41
35	27	19	11	3	-4	-12	-20	-28	-36	-43
40	26	18	10	2	-6	-14	-22	-29	-37	-45
45	25	17	9	1	-7	-15	-23	-31	-39	-47

WIND MPH	OUTSIDE AIR TEMPERATURE FARHENHEIT									
	0	-5	-10	-15	-20	-25	-30	-35	-40	-45
4	0	-5	-10	-15	-20	-25	-30	-35	-40	-45
6	-9	-14	-20	-25	-31	-36	-42	-47	-53	-58
8	-16	-21	-27	-33	-39	-45	-51	-57	-62	-68
10	-21	-27	-33	-40	-46	-52	-58	-64	-70	-77
12	-26	-32	-39	-45	-51	-58	-64	-71	-77	-83
14	-30	-36	-43	-50	-56	-63	-70	-76	-83	-89
16	-33	-40	-47	-54	-60	-67	-74	-81	-88	-95
18	-36	-43	-50	-57	-64	-71	-78	-85	-92	-99
20	-39	-46	-53	-60	-67	-75	-82	-89	-96	-103
22	-41	-48	-56	-63	-70	-78	85	-92	-99	-107
24	-43	-51	-58	-65	-73	-80	-88	-95	-102	-110
26	-45	-53	-60	-68	-75	-83	-90	-97	-105	-112
28	-47	-54	-62	-69	-77	-85	-92	-100	-107	-115
30	-48	-56	-64	-71	-79	-86	-94	-102	-109	-117
35	-51	-59	-67	-75	-82	-90	-98	-106	-114	-121
40	-53	-61	-69	-77	-85	-93	-101	-109	-116	-124
45	-55	-63	-71	-79	-86	-94	-102	-110	-118	-126

AVIATION ACRONYMS

ARROW - Documents required in the aircraft:
Airworthiness certificate.
Registration.
Radio station license.
Operating limitations.
Weight and balance.

CIGAR - Before takeoff checklist:
Controls (ailerons, elevator, rudder)
Instruments (flight instruments)
Gas (selector/gauges/mixture)
Attitude (trim/flaps)
Run-up (mags, carb-heat, gauges)

CIGFighTeR - Before takeoff checklist
Controls (ailerons, elevator, rudder)
Instruments (flight instruments)
Gas (selector/gauges/mixture)
Flaps (set)
Trim (takeoff)
Run-up (mags, carb-heat, gauges)

ANDS - Magnetic compass acceleration/turning error.
Accelerate North Decelerate South
Anticipate North Delay South

I'M SAFE - Pilot's personal checklist:
Illness
Medication
Stress
Alcohol
Fatigue
Emotions

GOOSE A CAT - Equipment required for day VFR:
Gas gauge
Oil temperature
Oil pressure
Seat belts
ELT transmitter
Altimeter
Compass
Airspeed indicator
Tachometer

APES - Equipment required for night VFR:
Anticollision lights
Position lights
Energy source
Spare fuses

TEST YOUR TAKEOFF - Takeoff roll checklist:
Time
Engine instruments
Strobe
Transponder

C-DART-GAS - Equipment required for IFR flight:
Clock with seconds
Directional gyro
Attitude indicator
Rate of turn indicator
Two-way nav/com radio
Generator of adequate capacity ,
Altimeter adjustable for pressure
Slip/skid indicator

EAST IS LEAST - WEST IS BEST
Subtract easterly magnetic variation
Add westerly magnetic variation.

HIGH TO LOW/(HOT TO COLD), LOOK OUT BELOW
Flying from an area of high pressure (or temperature) to an area
of low pressure (or temperature), actual altitude will be lower
than indicated altitude.

GUMP - Before landing checklist:
Gas (tank, selector, pump)
Undercarriage (landing gear, flaps)
Mixture (rich)
Propeller (high RPM)

6-6 RULE- IFR pilot currency requirements:
6 previous calendar months
6 approaches (all simulator okay)

FOUR 'C's - Procedure for lost VFR pilot:
Climb (weather permitting)
Conserve (maximum endurance)
Confess (ask for help)
Comply (follow ATC instructions)

6 'M's - Securing aircraft checklist:
Mixture (idle cut-off)
Movement (control lock)
Meter (hobbs)
Motion (chocks, tie-downs)
Mags (magnetos off)
Master (master switch off)

SIX 'T's - Final approach fix:
Time (start timer)
Turn (heading)
Twist (omni-bearing selector)
Throttle (adjust)
Talk (communicate)
Tires (landing gear down)

1-2-3 RULE - Weather requirements for not filing an alternate airport (IFR flight plan):
±1 hour of ETA
2,000' ceiling
3 miles visibility

CRAFT - Format for copying an ATC clearance:
Cleared to
Route
Altitude,
Frequency (departure control)
Transponder (squawk)

MEA - In the event of lost communications in IFR conditions, fly the highest altitude of, for the route segment being flown:
Minimum en route altitude
Expected as advised by ATC
Assigned by ATC

AVE-F - In the event of lost communications in IFR conditions, for the route segment being flown, fly the route that was last:
Assigned
Vectored
Expected or
Filed

TADS - Missed Approach /Go Around
Thrust-Climb Power
Attitude-Pitch for Climb
Drag- Gear Up, Flaps as required
Speed- Best Rate or V_{AC}

CALM STRAW - Mandatory reports to ATC at all times:
Climb -   unable 500 fpm climb or descend
Airspeed change of 10 KTS or 5% which ever is greater
Leaving - an assigned fix
Missed - approach
Safety - any thing affecting the safety of the flight
Time -   reaching an assigned fix
Radio -   failure of navigational or communications
Altitude - vacating one altitude for another
Weather -any unexpected weather

6 'A's - Initial approach segment checklist:
ATIS (obtain)
Altimeter (set),
Alignment (set DG)
Approach (how long, how low, which way)
Avionics (tune and identify)
Airspeed (slow to approach speed)

EAST IS ODD - VFR cruising altitudes:
Odd altitudes (plus 500') when flying easterly.
Even altitudes (plus 500') when flying westerly.

STEP ON THE BALL - Remember which rudder pressure is
required in order to recover from a slip or skid.

ICE-T - Airspeed Calculation
Indicated Airspeed
Calibrated Airspeed
Equivalent Airspeed
True Airspeed

Aviate/Navigate/Communicate - Order of Importance

SHARP-T - Procedure Turn Not Required
Straight-in
Holding Pattern
Arc (DME)
Radar Vectors
Procedure Turn (NoPT)
Timed Approaches (ATC)

PTA-(ENS) - Position Report
Position (Fix) - Mandatory or assigned by ATC.
Time Over Fix - Zulu time.
Altitude - (Flight Level)
Estimate to Next Fix - Next Mandatory.
Succeeding Fix - Mandatory or not.

DEPS - VOR 30 Day Check
Date
Error
Place
Signature

4 'C's - Missed Approach/Go-Around
Climb - Power/Pitch
Clean - Flaps, Gear
Cowl Flaps - Open
Communicate - Announce Missed Approach to ATC

Bank and Yank - Chandelles
Yank and Bank - Lazy '8's

True Virginians Make Delightful Company - Heading Order
True Heading +/-
Variation =
Magnetic Heading +/-
Deviation =
Compass Heading

IPAD - Initial Call to ATC
Identification
Position
Altitude
Destination or Intentions

TAPE - Required Aircraft Inspections
Transponder - 24 Months
Annual - 12 Months
Pitot/Static/Altimeter - 24 Months
Emergency Locator Transmitter - 12/24 Months

GUMP - Level Off/Cruise Check
Gas - Switch Tanks/Boost Pumps Off
Undercarriage - Cowl Flaps Closed
Mixture - Lean for Cruise
Props - Cruise RPM

8 Hours Bottle to Throttle - Minimum time after consuming alcoholic beverages before flying.

Tune-10/Turn-10 - Flying a DME arc, each time the CDI centers select another 10° on the OBS and make a 10° heading change.

(58)

ICAO AIRPORT IDENTIFIER COUNTRY PREFIX

A Solomon Islands, Nauru, Papua New Guinea

B Greenland, Iceland

C Haiti, Canada

D Algeria, Benin, Burkina, Ghana, Cote d'Ivoire, Nigeria, Niger, Togo

E Belgium, Germany, Finland, United Kingdom, Norway, Netherlands, Denmark, Luxembourg, Lithuania, Sweden, Belarus, Poland

F South Africa, Namibia, Botswana, Congo, Chad, Central African Republic, Cameroon, Zambia, Zaire, Comoros, Madagascar Angola, Mozambique, Seychelles, Zimbabwe, Swaziland, Lesotho

G Gambia, Sierra Leone, Guinea-Bissau, Morocco, Spain, Western Sahara, Cape Verde, Guinea, Mali

H Ethiopia, Burundi, Somalia, Djibouti, Egypt, Kenya, Jamahiriya, Rwanda, Sudan, Tanzania, Uganda

K United States

L Albania, Bulgaria, Cyprus, Croatia, Greece, Hungary, Italy, Slovenia, Czech Republic, Israel, Jordan, Austria, Portugal, Slovakia Bosnia/Herzegovina, Spain Yugoslavia, Romania, Switzerland, Macedonia, Gibraltar, Slovenia, France

M Dominican Republic, Belize Guatemala, Honduras, Jamaica, Mexico, Panama, Nicaragua, El Salvador, Haiti, Cuba, Cayman Is. Bahamas, Costa Rica

N Cook Islands, Fiji, Tonga, Kiribati, Tuvalu, Pago Pago, Samoa, French Polynesia, Tahiti, New Caledonia, New Zealand, Vanuatu

O Afghanistan, Bahrain, Saudi Arabia, Iran, Yemen Jordan, Kuwait, United Arab Emirates, Oman, Pakistan, Iraq, Syrian, Arab Republic, Qatar

P Alaska, Hawaii, New Zealand, Guam, Mariana Island, Guam, Micronesia, Sabanettan, Tinian, Rota Saipan, Agana, Micronesia, Peipeinimaru, Johnston Island, Marshall Islands, Wake Island

R Taiwan, Japan, Philippines,

S Argentina, Brazil, Chile, Ecuador, Falkland Islands, Paraguay, Colombia, Bolivia, Suriname, French Guinea, Peru, Uruguay, Guyana

T Antigua & Barbuda, Aruba, Barbados, Dominica, Puerto Rico, Saint Lucia, Netherlands Antilles, Trinidad and Tobago, Virgin Islands, St. Vincent & the Grenadines

U Kazakhstan, Kyrgyzstan, Azerbaijan, Russian, Federation, Armenia, Georgia, Ukraine, Moldova, Estonia, Belarus Latvia, Tajikistan, Uzbekistan

V India, Myanmar, Macao, Cambodia, Bangladesh, Hong Kong, Sri Lanka, Laos, Nepal, Maldives, Thailand, Vietnam

W Indonesia, Malaysia, Brunei, Darussalam, East Timor, Singapore

Y Australia, Christmas Is.

Z China, Korea

INTERNATIONAL CIVIL AIRCRAFT MARKINGS

A2	BOTSWANA	HS	THAILAND
A3	TONGA	HV	THE VATICAN
A40	OMAN	HZ	SAUDI ARABIA
A5	BHUTAN	I	ITALY
A6	UNITED ARAB	J2	DJIBOUTI
	EMIRATES	J3	GRENADA
A7	QATAR	J5	GUINEA BISSAU
A9C	BAHRAIN	J6	ST LUCIA
AP	PAKISTAN	J7	DOMINICA
B	CHINA/TAIWAN	J8	ST VINCENT
C-F, C-G	CANADA	JA	JAPAN
C2	NAURU	JY	JORDAN
C3	ANDORRA	LN	NORWAY
C5	GAMBIA	LQ, LV	ARGENTINA
C6	BAHAMAS	LX	LUXEMBOURG
C9	MOZAMBIQUE	LY	LITHUANIA
CC	CHILE	LZ	BULGARIA
CN	MOROCCO	MT	MONGOLIA
CP	BOLIVIA	N	UNITED STATES OF
CS	PORTUGAL		AMERICA
CU	CUBA	OB	PERU
CX	URUGUAY	OD	LEBANON
D	GERMANY	OE	AUSTRIA
D2	ANGOLA	OH	FINLAND
D4	CAPE VERDE ISLANDS	OK	CZECHIA
D6	COMORES ISLANDS	OM	SLOVAKIA
DQ	FIJI	OO	BELGIUM
E3	ERITREA	OY	DENMARK
EC	SPAIN	P	NORTH KOREA
EI	EIRE	P2	PAPUA NEW GUINEA
EK	ARMENIA	P4	ARUBA
EL	LIBERIA	PH	NETHERLANDS
EP	IRAN	PJ	NETHERLANDS
ER	MOLDOVA		ANTILLES
ES	ESTONIA	PK	INDONESIA
ET	ETHIOPIA	PP, PT	BRAZIL
EW	BELARUS	PZ	SURINAM
EX	KYRGYZSTAN	RA	RUSSIA
EY	TAJIKISTAN	RDPL	LAOS
EZ	TURKMENISTAN	RP	PHILIPPINE REPUBLIC
F	FRANCE	S2	BANGLADESH
G	UNITED KINGDOM	S5	SLOVENIA
GR	GEORGIA	S7	SEYCHELLES
H4	SOLOMON ISLANDS	S9	SAO TOME
HA	HUNGARY	SE	SWEDEN
HB	SWITZERLAND AND	SP	POLAND
	LIECHTENSTEIN	ST	SUDAN
HC	ECUADOR	SU	EGYPT
HH	HAITI	SX	GREECE
HI	DOMINICAN REPUBLIC	T2	TUVALU
HK	COLOMBIA	T3	KIRIBATI
HL	SOUTH KOREA	T7	SAN MARINO
HP	PANAMA	T9	BOSNIA-HERCEGOVINA
HR	HONDURAS	TC	TURKEY

TF	ICELAND	ZA	ALBANIA
TG	GUATEMALA	ZK	NEW ZEALAND
TI	COSTA RICA	ZP	PARAGUAY
TJ	UNITED REPUBLIC OF CAMEROON	ZS	SOUTH AFRICA
		3A	MONACO
TL	CENTRAL AFRICAN REPUBLIC	3B	MAURITIUS
		3C	EQUATORIAL GUINEA
TN	REPUBLIC OF CONGO	3D	SWAZILAND
TR	GABON	3X	GUINEA
TS	TUNISIA	4K	AZERBAIJAN
TT	CHAD	4L	GEORGIA
TU	IVORY COAST	4R	SRI LANKA
TY	BENIN	4U	UNITED NATIONS
TZ	MALI	4X	ISRAEL
UK	UZBEKISTAN	5A	LIBYA
UN	KAZAKHSTAN	5B	CYPRUS
UR	UKRAINE	5H	TANZANIA
V2	ANTIGUA	5N	NIGERIA
V3	BELIZE	5R	MADAGASCAR
V4	ST KITTS & NEVIS	5T	MAURITANIA
V5	NAMIBIA	5U	NIGER
V6	MICRONESIA	5V	TOGO
V7	MARSHALL ISLANDS	5W	WESTERN SAMOA (POLYNESIA)
V8	BRUNEI		
VH	AUSTRIA	5X	UGANDA
VN	VIETNAM	5Y	KENYA
VP-F	FALKLAND ISLANDS	6O	SOMALIA
VP-LA	ANGUILLA	6V	SENEGAL
VP-LM	MONTSERRAT	6Y	JAMAICA
VP-LV	VIRGIN ISLANDS	7O	YEMEN
VQ-T	TURKS & CAICOS ISLANDS	7P	LESOTHO
		7Q	MALAWI
VR-B	BERMUDA	7T	ALGERIA
VR-C	CAYMAN ISLANDS	8P	BARBADOS
VR-G	GIBRALTAR	8Q	MALDIVES
VR-H	HONG KONG	8R	GUYANA
VT-	INDIA	9A	CROATIA
XA-, XB-, XC-	MEXICO	9G	GHANA
XT	BURKINA FASO	9H	MALTA
XU	CAMBODIA	9J	ZAMBIA
XY	MYANMAR	9K	KUWAIT
YA	AFGHANISTAN	9L	SIERRA LEONE
YI	IRAQ	9M	MALAYSIA
YJ	VANUATU	9N	NEPAL
YK	SYRIA	9Q	ZAIRE
YL	LATVIA	9U	BURUNDI
YN	NICARAGUA	9V	SINGAPORE
YR	ROMANIA	9XR	RWANDA
YS	EL SALVADOR	9Y	TRINIDAD & TOBAGO
YU	YUGOSLAVIA		
YV	VENEZUELA		
Z	ZIMBABWE		
Z3	MACEDONIA		

WORLD TIME ZONES

LOCAL TIME ZONE	CONVERT TO UTC	CITY, COUNTRY *Observes Daylight Time
GMT- Greenwich Mean Time UTC-Universal Coordinated Time	+0	London, England*, Ireland* Casablanca, Morocco
WAT - West Africa Time	+1:00	Azores, Cape Verde Island
	+2:00	Antarctica*
	+3:00	Brazil*, Argentina, Greenland*
	+3:30	Canada Newfoundland*
AST - Atlantic Standard Time	+4:00	Venezuela, Barbados, Puerto Rico, Bolivia, Aruba
EST - Eastern Standard Time	+5:00	New York* , Jamaica, Cuba*, Colombia, Peru
CST - Central Standard Time	+6:00	Mexico City, Mexico Chicago, IL USA* Saskatchewan, Canada
MST - Mountain Standard Time	+7:00	Edmonton Canada* Denver, CO USA*
PST - Pacific Standard Time	+8:00	Vancouver, Canada* Los Angeles, CA USA*
YST - Yukon Standard Time	+9:00	Anchorage, AK USA*
HST - Hawaii Standard Time	+10:00	Honolulu, HI USA
NT - Nome Standard Time	+11:00	Nome, AK USA, Midway Is.
IDLW-International Date Line West	+12:00	
CET - Central European Time FWT - French WinterTime MET - Middle EuropeanTime SWT - Swedish WinterTime	-1:00	France*, Germany* Netherlands*, Belgium* Spain*, Italy*, Sweeden*, Switzerland*, Norway*
EET - Eastern European - USSR Zone 1	-2:00	Greece*, Finland*, Turkey*, Iserial*, Egypt*, South Africa
BT- Baghdad, USSR Zone 2	-3:00	Russia, Kuwait, Kenya, Iraq* Riyadh, Saudi Arabia
	-3:30	Terhan, Iran
ZP4 - USSR Zone 3	-4:00	
	-4:30	Alfganistan
ZP5 - USSR Zone 4	-5:00	Kyrgyzstan*
	-5:30	Bombay, India, Sri Lanka
ZP6 - USSR Zone 5	-6:00	Kazakhstan*, Tajikistan
	-6:30	Myanmar
ZP6 - USSR Zone 6	-7:00	Bangkok, Thailand
CCT - China Coast/Entire Country, - USSR Zone 7	-8:00	China, Singapore, Taiwan, Hong Kong, WestAustralia
JST - Japan Standard,	-9:00	Tokyo, Japan
	-9:30	Adelaide, Australia*
EAST - East Australian Standard	-10:00	Sydney, Australia*
	-11:00	Soloman Islands
	-11:30	Norfolk Island
IDLE-International Date Line East NZT - New Zealand Time	-12:00	Auckland, New Zealand* Fiji, Marshall Islands

FREQUENCY SPECTRUM

1 hertz (Hz)	1 cycle per second
15-20,000 Hz	Audio Frequencies
30-15,000 Hz	Normal Human Hearing Range
3-30 Hz	Extremely Low Frequency e.l.f.
30-300 Hz	Ultra Low Frequency u.l.f.
3-30 kHz	Very Low Frequency v.l.f.
30 kHz - 30,000 Mhz	Radio Frequencies
30 - 300 kHz	Low Frequencies l.f.
30-535 kHz	Marine Comm. & Navigation, Aero Nav.
300 - 3,000 kHz	Medium Frequencies MF
535-1705 kHz	AM Broadcast Bands
1800-2,000 kHz	Amateur Band, 160 meter
3-30 MHz	High Frequencies HF
30-300 MHz	Very High Frequencies VHF
30-50 MHz	Police, Fire, Forest, Highway, Railroad
50-54 MHz	Amateur Band, 6 Meter
54-72 MHz	TV Channels 2 to 4
72-76 MHz	Government, Marker Beacons 75 MHz
76-88 MHz	TV Channels 5 and 6
88-108 MHz	FM Broadcast Band
108.10 - 111.95	ILS Localizers
108.0 - 117.95	VORs
108-118 MHz	Aeronautical Navigation, VOR, LOC
118-136 MHz	Civil Communications Band
148-174 MHz	Government
144-148 MHz	Amateur Band, 2 Meter
174-216 MHz	TV Channels 7 to 13
216-470 MHz	Amateur, Government, CB Band, Fixed or Mobile Aernautical Navigation
220-225 MHz	Amateur Band, 1.25 Meter
329.15-335.00	Glide Slope
225-400 MHz	Military
420-450 MHz	Amateur Band, 0.7 Meter
462.55-563.2 MHz	Citizens Band Class A
300-3,000 MHz	Ultra High Frequency UHF
470-806 MHz	TV Channels 14 to 69
806-890 MHz	Cellular Telephone
890-3000 MHz	Aero Navigation, Amateur Bands
1,300-1,600 MHz	Radar Band
3,000-30,000 MHz	Super High Frequencies, Amateur Bands, Radio Navigation
30,000 MHz - 300 Ghz	Extra High Frequency (WX Radar)
30-0.76μm	Infared Light and Heat
0.39-0.76μm	Ultraviolet Light
0.032-0.0001 μm	X-rays
0.00001-0.0000006 μm	Gamma Rays
0.0005 angstroms	Cosmic Rays

VOR TEST FREQUENCIES (VOT)

Akron, OH	CAK	110.6		Long Beach, CA	LGB	113.9
Albuquerque, NM	ABQ	111.0		Los Angeles, CA	LAX	113.9
Anchorage, AK	ANC	111.0		Louisville, KY	SDF	111.0
Atlanta, GA	ATL	111.0		Medford	MFR	117.2
Bakersfield, CA	BFL	111.2		Memphis, TN	MEM	111.0
Bangor ME	BGR	111.0		Miami, FL	MIA	112.0
Bedford MA	BED	110.0		Midland, TX	MAF	108.2
Birmingham, AL	BHM	110.0		Milwaukee, WI	MKE	109.0
Boise, ID	BOI	116.7		Minneapolis, MN	MSP	111.0
Boston, MA	BOS	111.0		N. Las Vegas, NV	VGT	108.2
Bradley CT	BDL	111.4		Nashville, TN	BNA	108.6
Bridgeport CT	BDR	109.25		New Orleans LA	NEW	111.0
Brunswick GA	BQK	111.0		Oklahoma City	OKC	108.8
Centennial, CO	APA	108.2		Palm Beach, FL	PBI	109.0
Charleston AFB, SC	CHS	111.0		Phoenix, AZ	PHX	109.0
Charlotte, NC	CLT	112.0		Portland	HIO	115.2
Chicago, IL	MDW	111.0		Portland ME	PWM	111.0
Chicago, IL	ORD	112.0		Portland OR	PDX	111.0
Cincinnati, OH	LUK	108.4		Prescott	PRC	110.0
Cleveland, OH	CLE	110.4		Sacramento, CA	SAC	111.4
Colorado Springs	COS	110.4		Saint Louis, MO	STL	111.0
Columbus, OH	CMH	111.0		Saint Paul, MN	STP	114.4
Compton, CA	CPM	113.9		Salt Lake UT	SLC	111.0
Dallas, TX	DAL	113.3		San Antonio, TX	SAT	110.4
Datona Beach, FL	DAB	111.0		San Diego, CA	SDM	109.0
Davenport, IA	DVN	111.8		San Diego CA	SAN	109.0
Dayton, OH	DAY	111.0		San Diego CA	MYF	109.0
Denver, CO	DEN	111.0		San Francisco, CA	SFO	111.0
Des Moines, IA	DSM	109.2		Santa Ana CA	SNA	110.0
Detroit	DTW	109.8		Santa Monica, CA	SMO	113.9
Detroit City, MI	DET	111.6		Savannah, GA	SAV	111.0
Detroit, MI	YIP	112.0		Seattle	BFI	108.6
El Cajon, CA	SEE	110.0		Seattle	SEA	117.5
El Paso, TX	ELP	111.0		Shreveport la	SHV	108.2
Ft Worth, TX	FTW	108.2		Sidney, OH	I12	111.0
Ft. Wayne, IN	FWA	111.0		Smyrna, TN	MQY	110.2
Groton CT	GON	110.25		Spirit/St. Louis	SUS	112.2
Hartford CT	HFD	108.2		Spokane	GEG	109.6
Hawthorne, CA	HHR	113.9		Spokane	SFF	114.0
Hickory, NC	HKY	110.0		Tallahassee, FL	TLH	111.0
Houston, TX	HOU	111.6		Tampa, FL	TPA	111.0
Huntsville, AL	HSV	111.0		Topeka, KS	FOE	111.0
Indianapolis, IN	IND	111.8		Torrance CA	TOA	113.9
Jacksonville, FL	JAX	111.0		Tulsa, OK	TUL	109.0
Jacksonville, MS	JAN	111.0		Vero Beach, FL	VRB	111.0
JeffersonCty MO	JEF	112.0		Washington DC	DCA	109.4
Kansas City, MO	MKC	108.6		Wichita, KS	ICT	114.0
Knoxville, TN	TYS	112.0		Worcester MA	ORH	108.2

STANDARD ATMOSPHERE (ISA)					
Altitude Feet	Temp F°	Temp C°	Pressure in. Hg.	Pressure Mb	Speed of Sound KTS
0	59.0	15.0	29.92	1013.25	661.7
1000	55.4	13.0	28.86	977.16	659.5
2000	51.9	11.0	27.82	942.13	657.2
3000	48.3	9.1	26.82	908.20	654.9
4000	44.7	7.1	25.84	875.13	652.6
5000	41.2	5.1	24.90	843.18	650.3
6000	37.6	3.1	23.98	812.04	647.9
7000	34.0	1.1	23.09	781.18	645.6
`8000	30.5	-0.8	22.22	752.71	643.3
9000	26.9	-2.8	21.39	724.32	640.9
10,000	23.3	-4.8	20.58	696.94	638.6
15,000	5.5	-14.7	16.89	571.94	626.7
20,000	-12.3	-24.6	13.75	466.00	614.6
22,000	-19.3	-28.5	12.60	428.33	609.4
24,000	-26.5	-32.5	11.60	393.17	607.0
25,000	-30.2	-34.5	11.10	375.87	602.2
26,000	-33.5	-36.4	10.6	360.40	599.5
28,000	-40.8	-40.4	9.74	329.87	594.5
30,000	-48.0	-44.4	8.88	301.48	589.5
35,000	-65.8	-54.3	7.04	238.42	576.6
*36,089	-69.7	-56.5	6.68	225.79	573.8
40,000	-69.7	-56.5	5.56	188.23	573.8
45,000	-69.7	-56.5	4.37	148.14	573.8
50,000	-69.7	-56.5	3.44	116.64	573.8
55,000	-69.7	-56.5	2.71	91.80	573.8
60,000	-69.7	-56.5	2.12	72.31	573.8
70,000	-69.7	-56.5	1.31	44.38	573.8
80,000	-69.7	-56.5	0.81	27.45	573.8
90,000	-56.6	-49.6	0.50	17.02	583.4
100,000	-40.1	-40.3	0.32	10.84	595.2

(65)

MACH TO TRUE AIRSPEED AT ISA										
Altitude	.50	.55	.60	.65	.70	.75	.80	.85	.90	.95	1.0
S. L.	331	364	397	430	463	496	529	562	596	629	662
1,000	330	363	396	429	462	495	528	561	594	627	660
2,000	329	361	394	427	460	493	526	558	591	624	657
3,000	328	360	393	426	458	491	524	557	589	622	655
4,000	327	359	392	424	457	490	522	555	587	620	653
5,000	325	358	390	423	455	488	520	553	585	618	650
6,000	324	356	389	421	454	486	518	551	583	616	648
7,000	323	355	387	420	452	485	516	549	581	614	646
8,000	322	354	386	418	450	483	515	547	579	611	643
9,000	321	353	385	417	449	481	513	545	577	609	641
10,000	320	351	383	415	447	479	511	543	575	607	639
11,000	318	350	381	413	445	477	509	540	572	604	636
12,000	317	349	380	412	444	476	507	539	570	602	634
13,000	316	347	378	410	442	473	505	536	568	600	631
14,000	315	346	377	409	440	472	503	535	566	598	629
15,000	313	344	376	407	438	470	501	532	564	595	626
16,000	312	343	374	406	437	468	499	530	562	593	624
17,000	311	342	372	404	434	466	498	528	559	590	621
18,000	310	340	371	403	433	464	495	526	557	588	619
19,000	309	339	370	401	431	462	493	524	554	585	616
20,000	308	338	369	400	430	461	492	522	553	584	615
22,000	305	336	366	397	427	458	488	518	549	580	610
24,000	303	333	363	393	424	454	484	514	545	575	605
26,000	300	330	360	390	420	450	480	510	540	570	600
28,000	298	327	357	387	417	446	476	506	536	565	595
30,000	295	325	354	384	413	443	472	502	531	561	590
32,000	293	322	351	380	409	439	468	497	526	556	585
34,000	290	319	348	377	406	435	464	493	522	551	580
36,000+	288	316	345	374	402	431	460	489	517	546	575

$$TAS = MACH \times 39\sqrt{273 + C} \qquad MACH = \frac{TAS}{39\sqrt{273 + C}}$$

V-SPEEDS

V_1	TAKEOFF DECISION SPEED
V_2	TAKEOFF SAFETY SPEED
V_A	DESIGN MANEUVERING SPEED
V_{AC}	MISSED APPROACH CLIMB SPEED
V_B	DESIGN SPEED FOR MAXIMUM GUST INTENSITY
V_C	DESIGN CRUISING SPEED
V_D	DESIGN DIVING SPEED
$V_{DF/MDF}$	DEMONSTRATED FLIGHT DIVING SPEED
V_F	DESIGN FLAP SPEED
V_{FS}	FLAP RETRACTION SPEED
$V_{FC/MFC}$	MAXIMUM SPEED FOR STABILITY CHARACTERISTICS
V_{FE}	MAXIMUM FLAP EXTENDED SPEED
V_H	MAXIMUM SPEED IN LEVEL FLIGHT WITH CONTINUOUS POWER
V_{LE}	MAXIMUM LANDING GEAR EXTENDED SPEED
V_{LO}	MAXIMUM LANDING GEAR OPERATING SPEED
V_{LOF}	LIFT-OFF SPEED
V_{MC}	MINIMUM CONTROL SPEED WITH THE CRITICAL ENGINE INOPERATIVE
V_{MCA}	AIR MINIMUM CONTROL SPEED
V_{MCG}	GROUND MINIMUM CONTROL SPEED
$V_{MO/MMO}$	MAXIMUM OPERATING LIMIT SPEED
V_{MU}	MINIMUM UNSTICK SPEED
V_{NE}	NEVER EXCEED SPEED
V_{NO}	MAXIMUM STRUCTURAL CRUISING SPEED
V_{PW}	MAXIMUM PILOT WINDOW OPEN SPEED
V_R	ROTATION SPEED
V_{REF}	REFERENCE SPEED
V_S	STALLING SPEED/MINIMUM CONTROLLABLE STEADY FLIGHT SPEED
V_{S1}	STALLING SPEED/MINIMUM STEADY FLIGHT SPEED IN A SPECIFIED CONFIGURATION
V_{SO}	STALLING SPEED/MINIMUM CONTROLLABLE STEADY FLIGHT SPEED IN THE LANDING CONFIGURATION
V_{SSE}	STALL SPEED SINGLE ENGINE
V_{TOS}	TAKEOFF SAFETY SPEED
V_{TOSS}	TAKEOFF SAFETY SPEED FOR CATEGORY A ROTORCRAFT
V_{WW}	WINDSHIELD WIPER OPERATING SPEED
V_X	BEST ANGLE OF CLIMB AIRSPEED
V_{XSE}	BEST ANGLE OF CLIMB AIRSPEED W/ONE ENGINE INOPERATIVE
V_Y	BEST RATE OF CLIMB AIRSPEED
V_{YSE}	BEST RATE OF CLIMB AIRSPEED WITH ONE ENGINE INOPERATIVE

AVIATION ABBREVIATIONS

A	AIRPORT·AREA, AVAILABLE, ARM, ALERT AREA, AMBER
A/A	AIR TO AIR
AAA	AIRPORT ADVISORY AREA -10 MILE RADIUS OF A FSS WITHOUT A CONTROL TOWER
AADC	APPROACH AND DEPARTURE CONTROL
AAC	ALASKAN AIR COMMAND
AAI	ANGLE OF APPROACH INDICATOR
AAL	ABOVE AERODROME LEVEL
AAS	AIRPORT ADVISORY SERVICE-APT W/O TOWER
AATM	AT ALL TIMES
AAU	AUTHORIZED APPROACH (UNICOM)
AAWF	AUXILIARY AVIATION WEATHER FACILITY
AB	AIR BASE
ABM	ABEAM
ABN	AERODROME BEACON
AC	ADVISORY CIRCULAR, ALTERNATING CURRENT, AIR CARRIER
A/C	APPROACH CONTROL, AIRCRAFT
ACA	ARCTIC CONTROL AREA
ACARS	AIRCRAFT COMMUNICATIONS ADDRESSING & REPORTING SYSTEM
ACAS	AIRBORNE COLLISION AVOIDANCE SYSTEM
ACCEL	ACCELEROMETER
ACFT	AIRCRAFT
AD	AIRWORTHINESS DIRECTIVE
A/D	ANALOG TO DIGITAL

ADA	AERODROME ADVISORY AREA
ADC	AIR DATA COMPUTER
ADCUS	ADVISE CUSTOMS
ADF	AUTOMATIC DIRECTION FINDER
ADG	AIR DRIVEN GENERATOR
ADI	ATTITUDE DIRECTOR INDICATOR
ADIZ	AIR DEFENSE IDENTIFICATION ZONE
ADR	ADVISORY ROUTE
ADS	AIR DATA SYSTEMS
AEIS	AERONAUTICAL ENROUTE INFORMATION SERVICE
AER	APPROACH END RUNWAY
AF	AUDIO FREQUENCY
AFC	AREA FORECAST CENTER
AFCS	AUTOMATIC FLIGHT CONTROL SYSTEM
A/FD	AIRPORT FACILITIES DIRECTORY
AFFF	AQUEOUS FILM FORMING FOAM
AFH	ABOVE FIELD HEIGHT
AFIS	AERODROME FLIGHT INFORMATION SERVICE
AFL	ABOVE FIELD LEVEL
AFSS	AUTOMATED FLIGHT SERVICE STATION
AFT	AFTER, REARWARD
AGL	ABOVE GROUND LEVEL
AGNIS	AZIMUTH GUIDANCE NOSE-IN-STAND
AI	ATTITUDE INDICATOR
A/I	ANTI-ICE
AIM	AIRMAN'S INFORMATION MANUAL
AIRMET	AIRMAN'S METEOROLOGICAL INFORMATION

AIS	AERONAUTICAL INFORMATION SERVICE	AR	ATLANTIC ROUTE
ALNOT	ALERT NOTICE	ARC	AUTOMATIC RADIAL CENTERING
ALS	APPROACH LIGHTING SYSTEM, AUTOMATIC LANDING SYSTEM	ARFF	AIRCRAFT RESCUE AND FIRE FIGHTING
ALSF(1)	HIGH INTENSITY APPROACH LIGHTING SYSTEM WITH SEQUENCED FLASHING LIGHTS	ARINC	AERONAUTICAL RADIO INC.
		ARP	AIRPORT REFERENCE POINT
		ARSR	AIR ROUTE SURVEILLANCE RADAR
ALSF2	ALSF WITH RED SIDE ROW LIGHTS THE LAST 1,000 FEET	ARTC	AIR ROUTE TRAFFIC CONTROL
AM	AMPLITUDE MODULATED, ANTEMERIDIAN	ARTCC	AIR ROUTE TRAFFIC CONTROL CENTER
		ARTS	AUTOMATED RADAR TERMINAL SYSTEM
AMA	AREA MINIMUM ALTITUDE	AS, A/S	AIRSPEED
AME	AVIATION MEDICAL EXAMINER	ASDA	ACCELERATE STOP DISTANCE AVAILABLE
AMEL	AIRPLANE MULTI-ENGINE LAND	ASEL	AIRPLANE SINGLE-ENGINE LAND, ALTITUDE SELECT
AMES	AIRPLANE MULTI-ENGINE SEA	ASES	AIRPLANE SINGLE-ENGINE SEA
AMOS	AUTOMATIC METEOROLOGICAL OBSERVING STATION	ASI	AIR SPEED INDICATOR
		ASL	ABOVE SEA LEVEL
		ASOS	AUTOMATED SURFACE OBSERVATION SYSTEM
AMP	AMPERE, AMPLIFY		
ANN	ANNUNCIATOR	ASR	AIRPORT SURVEILLANCE RADAR
ANT	ANTENNA		
AOA	ANGLE OF ATTACK	ASRP	AVIATION SAFETY REPORTING PROGRAM
AOE	AIRPORT OF ENTRY		
AOPA	AIRCRAFT OWNERS & PILOTS ASSOCIATION	ATA	ACTUAL TIME OF ARRIVAL
A&P	AIRFRAME AND POWERPLANT	ATC	AIR TRAFFIC CONTROL, APPROVED TYPE CERTIFICATE
A/P	AUTOPILOT		
APAP	APPROACH PATH ALIGNMENT PANELS	ATCAA	ATC ASSIGNED AIRSPACE
APAPI	ABBREVIATED PRECISION APPROACH PATH INDICATOR	ATCT	AIR TRAFFIC CONTROL TOWER
		ATCC	AIR TRAFFIC CONTROL CENTER
APC	APPROACH CONTROL	ATCRBS	AIR TRAFFIC CONTROL RADAR BEACON SYSTEM
APT	AIRPORT		
APU	AUXILIARY POWER UNIT		

ATD	ACTUAL TIME OF DEPARTURE	BUTE	BENT UP TRAILING EDGE
ATF	AERODROME TRAFFIC FREQUENCY	C	CELSIUS, CENTER, CTAF, CLEARANCE
ATIS	AUTOMATED TERMINAL INFORMATION SERVICE	CAA	CIVIL AERONAUTICS ADMINISTRATION
ATP	AIRLINE TRANSPORT PILOT	CAB	CIVIL AERONAUTICS BOARD
AT-VASI	ABBREVIATED TEE-VASI	CADIZ	CANADIAN AIR DEFENSE ZONE
AUTOB	AUTOMATIC OBSERVING STATION	CAF	CLEARED AS FILED
AUW	ALL-UP WEIGHT	CAP	CIVIL AIR PATROL
AUX	AUXILIARY	CARF	CENTRAL ALTITUDE RESERVATION FUNCTION
AVASI	ABBREVIATED VASI		
AVGAS	AVIATION GASOLINE	CAS	CALIBRATED AIR SPEED
AWOS	AUTOMATED WEATHER OBSERVING SYSTEM	CAT	CATEGORY
AWRS	AUTOMATIC WEATHER REPORTING STATION	CAWS	COMMON AVIATION WEATHER SUB-SYSTEM
AWS	AURAL WARNING SYSTEM	CB	CITIZENS BAND, CIRCUIT BREAKER
AWW	ALERT SEVERE WEATHER WATCH	CCA	CONTINENTAL CONTROL AREA
AZM	AZIMUTH	CD	CLEARANCE DELIVERY
B	BEACON AVAILABLE	CDI	COURSE DEVIATION INDICATOR
B+	JET B FUEL W/ANTI-ICING INHIBITOR (FREEZING PT. - 76°F)	CELNAV	CELESTIAL NAVIGATION
B/A	BANK ANGLE	CEPAC	CENTRAL EASTERN PACIFIC ROUTES (US TO HAWAII)
BC	BACK COURSE		
BCM	BACK COURSE MARKER	CFA	CONTROLLED FIRING AREA
BHP	BRAKE HORSE POWER		
BFR	BIENNIAL FLIGHT REVIEW	CFI	CERTIFIED FLIGHT INSTRUCTOR
BFO	BEAT FREQUENCY OSCILLATOR	CFII	CERTIFIED FLIGHT INSTRUCTOR-INSTRUMENT
BGI	BASIC GROUND INSTRUCTOR	CFIT	CONTROLLED FLIGHT INTO TERRAIN
BIT	BUILT IN TEST	CG	CENTER OF GRAVITY
BITE	BUILT IN TEST EQUIPMENT	CH	COURSE HEADING, CRITICAL HEIGHT
BM	BACK MARKER		
BS	BROADCAST STATION (COMMERCIAL)	CHT	CYLINDER HEAD TEMPERATURE

CL	RUNWAY CENTERLINE LIGHTS, CENTER OF LIFT, CLOSED	DG (D/G)	DIRECTIONAL GYRO
CLNC	CLEARANCE	DH	DECISION HEIGHT
CLNC DEL	CLEARANCE DELIVERY	DME	DISTANCE MEASURING EQUIPMENT
COMLO	COMPASS LOCATOR	DME/P	PRECISION DME
COMM	COMMUNICATIONS	DOD	DEPARTMENT OF DEFENSE
CONTRAILS	CONDENSATION TRAILS	DOT	DEPARTMENT OF TRANSPORTATION
COORD	COORDINATES	DOT-1	TRANSPORT ONE - SECRETARY OF TRANSPORTATION
COP	CHANGE OVER POINT		
Cpt	CLEARANCE (PRE-TAXI PROCEDURE)	DPC	DEPARTURE CONTROL
CPU	CENTRAL PROCESSING UNIT	DPCR	DEPARTURE PROCEDURE
C/R	COUNTER ROTATING	DR	DEAD RECKONING, DIRECT
CRM	COCKPIT RESOURCE MANAGEMENT	DSB	DOUBLE SIDE BAND
CRP	COMPULSORY REPORTING POINT	DTLN	INTERNATIONAL DATE LINE
CRT	CATHODE-RAY TUBE	DUAT	DIRECT USER ACCESS TERMINAL SYSTEM
CT	CONTROL TOWER		
CTA	CONTROL AREA	DVFR	DEFENSE VFR
CTAF	COMMON TRAFFIC ADVISORY FREQUENCY	DVOR	DOPPLER VOR
CVFP	CHARTED VISUAL FLIGHT PROCEDURE	E6B	FLIGHT COMPUTER
		EAC	EXPECTED APPROACH CLEARANCE
CVR	COVER, COCKPIT VOICE RECORDER	EADI	ELECTRONIC ATTITUDE DIRECTOR INDICATOR
CW	CONTINUOUS WAVE	EARTS	ENROUTE AUTOMATED RADAR TRACKING SYSTEM
CWA	CENTER WEATHER ADVISORY		
CWSU	CENTER WEATHER SERVICE UNIT	EAS	EQUIVALENT AIR SPEED
CYL	CYLINDER	EAT	EXPECTED APPROACH TIME
DA	DENSITY ALTITUDE, DECISION ALTITUDE	EDCT	EXPECT DEPARTURE CLEARANCE TIME
dB	DECIBEL	EET	ESTIMATED ELAPSED TIME
DC	DIRECT CURRENT, DRY CHEMICAL	EFAS	ENROUTE FLIGHT ADVISORY SERVICE
DDT	DUAL-DOUBLE TANDEM AXLE	EFIS	ELECTRONIC FLIGHT INSTRUMENT SYSTEM
DEL	DELIVERY		
DEWIZ	DISTANT EARLY WARNING IDENTIFICATION ZONE	EFC	EXPECT FURTHER CLEARANCE (TIME)
		EGME	ETHYLENE GLYCOL METHYL ETHER (FUEL ADDITIVE)
DF	DIRECTION FINDER		

EGT	EXHAUST GAS TEMPERATURE	FAS	FINAL APPROACH SEGMENT
EHAC	ENROUTE HIGH ALTITUDE CHART	FBO	FIXED BASE OPERATION
ELAC	ENROUTE LOW ALTITUDE CHART	FCC	FEDERAL COMMUNICATIONS COMMISSION
ELT	EMERGENCY LOCATOR TRANSMITTER	FCP	FINAL CONTROL POINT
EMS	EMERGENCY MEDICAL SERVICE	FD	FLIGHT DIRECTOR
E-MSAW	ENROUTE MINIMUM SAFE ALTITUDE WARNING	FDC	FLIGHT DIRECTOR COMPUTER, FLIGHT DATA CENTER
EPR	ENGINE PRESSURE RATIO	FDR	FLIGHT DATA RECORDER
EST	ESTIMATE	FE	FLIGHT ENGINEER
ET	ELAPSED TIME	FF	FUEL FLOW
ETA	ESTIMATED TIME OF ARRIVAL	FFC	FOR FURTHER CLEARANCE
ETD	ESTIMATED TIME OF DEPARTURE	FIC	FLIGHT INFORMATION CENTER
ETE	ESTIMATED TIME ENROUTE	FIR	FLIGHT INFORMATION REGION
ETP	EQUAL TIME POINT	FIS	FLIGHT INFORMATION SERVICE
EXEC-1	PRESIDENT ON BOARD CIVIL AIRCRAFT	FL	FLIGHT LEVEL
EXEC-1F	PRESIDENTS FAMILY ON BOARD CIVIL AIRCRAFT	FLIP	FLIGHT INFORMATION PUBLICATION
EXEC-2	VICE PRESIDENT ON BOARD CIVIL AIRCRAFT	FLWIS	FLOOD WARNING ISSUED
		FLTWO	FLIGHT WATCH OUTLET
EXEC-2F	VICE PRESIDENT'S FAMILY ON BOARD CIVIL AIRCRAFT	FM	FREQUENCY MODULATION, FAN MARKER, FROM
EX LOC	EXPANDED LOCALIZER	FMS	FLIGHT MANAGEMENT SYSTEM
F	FAHRENHEIT, SEQUENTIAL FLASHING LIGHTS	FOB	FUEL ON BOARD
		FOD	FOREIGN OBJECT DAMAGE
FAA	FEDERAL AVIATION ADMINISTRATION	FPM	FEET PER MINUTE
FAC	FACILITY, FINAL APPROACH COURSE	FPR	FLIGHT PLANNED ROUTE
FAF	FINAL APPROACH FIX	FRC	FULL ROUTE CLEARANCE
FAP	FINAL APPROACH POINT	FREQ	FREQUENCY
		FS	FUSELAGE STATION
FAR	FEDERAL AVIATION REGULATION	FSDO	FLIGHT STANDARDS DISTRICT OFFICE

FSS	FLIGHT SERVICE STATION	HH	HIGH POWER NDB (>2,000 WATTS)
FUBAR	BEYOND ALL REPAIR	HI	HIGH INTENSITY LIGHTS
FWF	FIREWALL FORWARD		
FV	FLIGHT VISIBILITY, FORWARD VISIBILITY	HIALS	HIGH INTENSITY APPROACH LIGHT SYSTEM
FYI	FOR YOUR INFORMATION		
		HIBAL	HIGH ALTITUDE BALLOON
G	ACCELERATION OF GRAVITY FORCE, GUARDS ONLY	HIRL	HIGH INTENSITY RUNWAY EDGE LIGHTS
GA	GENERAL AVIATION, GRADIENT ANGLE, GO AROUND	HIWAS	HAZARDOUS IN-FLIGHT WEATHER ADVISORY SERVICE
G/A	GROUND TO AIR,	HOTAS	HANDS-ON-THROTTLE-AND-STICK
GADO	GENERAL AVIATION DISTRICT OFFICE	HP	HORSEPOWER
GC	GROUND CONTROL	hPa	HECTOPASCAL
GCA	GROUND CONTROLLED APPROACH	HSI	HORIZONTAL SITUATION INDICATOR, HOT SECTION INSPECTION
GMT	GREENWICH MEAN TIME		
GNSS	GLOBAL NAVIGATION SATELITE SYSTEM	HUD	HEAD-UP DISPLAY
		HURL	AIRSICK
GPH	GALLONS PER HOUR	HVOR	HIGH ALTITUDE VOR
GPI	GROUND POINT OF INTERCEPTION	Hz	HERTZ
GPS	GLOBAL POSITIONING SYSTEM	IA	INSPECTION AUTHORIZATION
GPWS	GROUND PROXIMITY WARNING SYSTEM	IAC	INSTRUMENT APPROACH CHART
GS	GLIDE SLOPE, GROUND SPEED	IAF	INITIAL APPROACH FIX
GWT	GROSS WEIGHT	IAP	INSTRUMENT APPROACH PROCEDURE
		IAPC	IAP CHART
H	HIGH, HEAVY, HAZARDS, HOLD, HIGH ALTITUDE NDB	IAS	INDICATED AIR SPEED
		IAW	IN ACCORDANCE WITH
		IB	INBOUND
HAA	HEIGHT ABOVE AIRPORT	ICAO	INTERNATIONAL CIVIL AVIATION ORGANIZATION
HAT	HEIGHT ABOVE TOUCHDOWN		
		ID	IDENTIFICATION
HDF	HF DIRECTION FINDING STATION	IDENT	IDENTIFY
		IF	INTERMEDIATE FIX
HDTA	HIGH DENSITY TRAFFIC AIRPORT	IFF	IDENTIFICATION FRIEND OR FOE
HF	HIGH FREQUENCY	IFR	INSTRUMENT FLIGHT RULES
"HG	INCHES OF MERCURY		

ILS	INSTRUMENT LANDING SYSTEM	KCAS	KNOTS CALIBRATED AIR SPEED
IM	INNER MARKER	KIAS	KNOTS INDICATED AIR SPEED
IMC	INSTRUMENT METEOR-OLOGICAL CONDITIONS	KTAS	KNOTS TRUE AIR SPEED
IMTA	INTENSIVE MILITARY TRAINING AREA	KT(S)	KNOT(S)
INBD	INBOUND, INBOARD	KVA	KILO VOLT AMPERES
INOP	INOPERATIVE	KW	KILOWATT
INP	IF NOT POSSIBLE	L	LOCATOR (COMPASS), LOW ALTITUDE
INS	INERTIAL NAVIGATION SYSTEM	*L	LIGHTING (PILOT CONTROLLED)
IOE	INITIAL OPERATING EXPERIENCE	LA	LIGHTER THAN AIR AIRSHIP
I/P	INPUT	LAAS	LOW ALTITUDE ALERT SYSTEM
IPC	ILLUSTRATED PARTS CATALOG	LAT	LATITUDE, LATERAL
IR	IFR MILITARY TRAINING ROUTE	LAWRS	LIMITED AVIATION WEATHER REPORTING STATION
IRAN	INSPECT AND REPAIR AS NECESSARY	LCD	LIQUID CRYSTAL DISPLAY
IRC	INSTRUMENT REMOTE CONTROLLER	LCL	LOCAL
		L/D	LIFT TO DRAG RATIO
ISA	INTERNATIONAL STANDARD ATMOSPHERE	L/D_{MAX}	POINT OF MAXIMUM LIFT TO DRAG RATIO
ITT	INTER-TURBINE TEMPERATURE	LDA	LOCALIZER-TYPE DIRECTIONAL AID
IVRS	INTERIM VOICE RESPONSE SYSTEM	LDG	LANDING
IVSI	INTERTIAL VERTICAL SPEED INDICATOR	LDI	LANDING DIRECTION INDICATOR
IVV	INSTANTANEOUS VERTICAL VELOCITY	LDIN	LEAD IN LIGHTING SYSTEM (SEQUENCED FLASHING LIGHTS)
J	JET ROUTE, JUMP	LED	LIGHT EMITTING DIODE
JATO	JET ASSISTED TAKEOFF	LF	LOW FREQUENCY
JB	JUNCTION BOX	LFM	LOW-POWERED FAN MARKER
JET A	KEROSENE-FREEZE POINT -40°F	LIM	LOCATOR INNER MARKER
JET A1	KEROSENE WITH ADDITIVE FREEZE POINT -58°	LIRL	LOW INTENSITY RUNWAY LIGHTS
		LLWAS	LOW LEVEL WIND SHEAR ALERT SYSTEM
K	CONTIGUOUS UNITED STATES	L/MF	LOW/MEDIUM FREQUENCY

LMM	LOCATOR MIDDLE MARKER		AIRSPEED, MINIMUM CROSSING ALTITUDE
LOC	ILS LOCALIZER, LOCATOR, LOCALLY	MDA	MINIMUM DESCENT ALTITUDE
LOFT	LINE ORIENTED FLIGHT TRAINING	MDH	MAJOR DAMAGE HISTORY
LOM	LOCATOR OUTER MARKER	MEA	MINIMUM ENROUTE ALTITUDE
LONG	LONGITUDE	MEF	MAXIMUM ELEVATION FIGURE
LOP	LINE OF POSITION		
LORAN	LONG RANGE RADIO AID TO NAVIGATION	MEHT	MINIMUM EYE HEIGHT OVER THRESHOLD
LOX	LIQUID OXYGEN	MEI	MULTI-ENGINE INSTRUMENT
LR	LEAD RADIAL		
LSALT	LOWEST SAFE ALTITUDE	MEL	MINIMUM EQUIPMENT LIST, MULTI-ENGINE LAND
LSB	LOWER SIDE BAND		
LTA	LIGHTER THAN AIR	MES	MULTI-ENGINE SEA
LVOR	LOW ALTITUDE VOR	METAR	AVIATION ROUTINE WEATHER REPORT
M	MACH, MINUTE, MODE, MOMENT, METERS	MF	MEDIUM FREQUENCY
		MFD	MULTI-FUNCTION DISPLAY
MAA	MAXIMUM AUTHORIZED ALTITUDE	MH	MAGNETIC HEADING, MEDIUM POWER HOMING NDB-50 WATTS
MAC	MEAN AERODYNAMIC CHORD		
MAG	MAGNETIC, MAGNETO	MHA	MINIMUM HOLDING ALTITUDE
MALS	MEDIUM INTENSITY APPROACH LIGHT SYSTEM	MHz	MEGAHERTZ
		MIALS	MEDIUM INTENSITY APPROACH LIGHT SYSTEM
MALSF	MEDIUM INTENSITY APPROACH LIGHT SYSTEM W/SEQUENCED FLASHING LIGHTS		
		MIC	MICROPHONE
		MIRL	MEDIUM INTENSITY RUNWAY EDGE LIGHTS
MALSR	MEDIUM INTENSITY APPROACH LIGHT SYSTEM WITH RAIL	MKR	MARKER BEACON
		ML	MIDDLE COMPASS LOCATOR
MASI	MACH AIRSPEED INDICATOR	MLG	MAIN LANDING GEAR
MAP	MISSED APPROACH POINT	MLS	MICROWAVE LANDING SYSTEM
		MLW	MAXIMUM LANDING WEIGHT
MAYDAY	INTERNATIONAL DISTRESS SIGNAL	MM	MIDDLE MARKER
MB	MARKER BEACON, MILLIBAR, MAGNETIC BEARING	MNPS	MINIMUM NAVIGATION PERFORMANCE SPECIFICATION AIRSPACE
MC	MAGNETIC COURSE		
MCA	MANEUVERING AT CRITICALLY SLOW		

MOA	MILITARY OPERATIONS AREA		PROCEDURE
MOCA	MINIMUM OBSTRUCTION CLEARANCE ALTITUDE	NAS	NATIONAL AIRSPACE SYSTEM
MODE C	AUTOMATIC ALTITUDE REPORTING	NASA	NATIONAL AERONAUTICS & SPACE AMINISTRATION
MOGAS	AUTO GAS USED FOR AIRCRAFT	NAT	NORTH ATLANTIC TRAFFIC
MORA	MINIMUM OFF-ROUTE ALTITUDE	NBAA	NATIONAL BUSINESS AIRCRAFT ASSOCIATION
MP	MANIFOLD PRESSURE	NCRP	NON-COMPULSORY REPORTING POINT
MPH	MILES PER HOUR		
MPS	METERS PER SECOND	NDB	NON-DIRECTIONAL RADIO BEACON
MRA	MINIMUM RECEPTION ALTITUDE	NDH	NO DAMAGE HISTORY
MSA	MINIMUM SECTOR ALTITUDE	NDT	NON-DESTRUCTIVE TESTING
MSAW	MINIMUM SAFE ALTITUDE WARNING	NFCT	NON-FEDERAL CONTROL TOWER
MSL	MEAN SEA LEVEL	NLG	NOSE LANDING GEAR
MTA	MILITARY TRAINING AREA	NM	NAUTICAL MILES
MTCA	MINIMUM TERRAIN CLEARANCE ALTITUDE	NMAC	NEAR MID-AIR COLLISION
MTOW	MAXIMUM TAKEOFF WEIGHT	NOAA	NATIONAL OCEANIC AND ATMOSPHERIC ADMINISTRATION
MTR	MILITARY TRAINING ROUTE	NOPT	NO PROCEDURE TURN REQUIRED
MUX	MULTIPLEXER	NOS	NATIONAL OCEAN SURVEY
MVA	MINIMUM VECTORING ALTITUDE	NOTAM	NOTICE TO AIRMEN
		NSSFC	NATIONAL SEVERE STORMS FORECAST CENTER, NWS
N	NEGATIVE, NIGHT		
N_1	LOW PRESSURE COMPRESSOR (FAN SPEED)	NTSB	NATIONAL TRANSPORTATION SAFETY BOARD
N_2	HIGH PRESSURE COMPRESSOR SPEED (CORE SPEED)	NTSD	LIGHT SYSTEM FAILING TO MEET FAA STANDARDS
NA	NOT AUTHORIZED, NOT AVAILABLE	NWS	NATIONAL WEATHER SERVICE
N/A	NOT APPLICABLE		
NAF	NAVAL AIR FIELD	O2	OXYGEN
NAR	NORTH AMERICAN ROUTES	OAT	OUTSIDE AIR TEMPERATURE
NARC	NORTH ATLANTIC ROUTE CHART	OB	OUTBOUND
NAP	NOISE ABATEMENT		

OBS	OBSTACLE, OMNI-BEARING SELECTOR	PARL	PREFERENTIAL ARRIVAL ROUTE
OCA	OCEANIC CONTROL AREA	PATWAS	PILOT'S AUTOMATIC TELEPHONE WEATHER ANSWERING SERVICE
OCH	OBSTACLE CLEARANCE HEIGHT	PAX	PASSENGER
OCL	OBSTRUCTION CLEARANCE LIMIT	PBCT	PROPOSED BOUNDARY CROSSING TIME
ODALS	OMNI-DIRECTIONAL APPROACH LIGHT SYSTEM	PC	PILOTAGE CHART, POSITIVE CONTROL
OH	OVERHAUL	PCA	POSITIVE CONTROL AREA
OLS	OPTICAL LANDING SYSTEM	PCL	PILOT CONTROLLED LIGHTING
OM	OUTER MARKER	PCU	POWER CONTROL UNIT
OP	OPERATION, OPERATE	PCW	PREVIOUSLY COMPLIED WITH
O/P	OUTPUT		
OPT	OPTIONAL	PCZ	POSITIVE CONTROL ZONE
OPS	OPERATIONS	PDAR	PREFERENTIAL DEPARTURE AND ARRIVAL ROUTE
O/R	ON REQUEST		
OSV	OCEAN STATION VESSEL		
O/T	OTHER TIMES	PDR	PREFERENTIAL DEPARTURE ROUTE
OTR	OCEANIC TRANSITION ROUTE	PDW	PRIORITY DELAYED WEATHER
OTS	OUT OF SERVICE		
OX1	HIGH PRESSURE OXYGEN	P-FACTOR	ASYMMETRICAL THRUST
OX2	LOW PRESSURE OXYGEN	PIBAL	PILOT BALLOON OBSERVATION
OXY	OXYGEN	PIC	PILOT IN COMMAND
		PIO	PILOT INDUCED OSCILLATIONS
P	PROHIBITED AREA		
P2(L)(R)	2 PAPI LIGHTS (LEFT OR RIGHT SIDE OFF RUNWAY)	PIREP	PILOT WEATHER REPORT
		PLASI	PULSATING VISUAL APPROACH SLOPE INDICATOR
P4(L)(R)	4 PAPI LIGHTS (LEFT OR RIGHT SIDE OFF RUNWAY)		
		PM	POSTMERIDIAN
PA	PRESSURE ALTITUDE	PNF	PILOT NOT FLYING
PAJA	PARACHUTE JUMPING ACTIVITIES	PNR	PRIOR NOTICE REQUIRED
PAN-PAN	INTERNATIONAL DISTRESS SIGNAL	POB	PERSONS ON BOARD (INCLUDING CREW)
PAPI	PRECISION APPROACH PATH INDICATOR	POH	PILOT'S OPERATING HANDBOOK
PAR	PRECISION APPROACH RADAR, PARALLEL	PPH	POUNDS PER HOUR (FUEL)

PPO	PRIOR PERMISSION ONLY	RC	REVERSE COURSE
PPR	PRIOR PERMISSION REQUIRED	RCC	RESCUE COORDINATION CENTER
PRA	PRECISION RADAR APPROACH	RCL	RUNWAY CENTERLINE
PROP	PROPELLER (AIRCRAFT)	RCLM	RUNWAY CENTERLINE MARKING
Ps	STATIC PRESSURE	RCLS	RUNWAY CENTERLINE LIGHT SYSTEM
PSI	POUNDS PER SQUARE INCH	RCO	REMOTE COMMUNICATIONS OUTLET
PSID	PSI DIFFERENTIAL		
PSI(L)(R)	PVASI (LEFT OR RIGHT SIDE OF RUNWAY)	R&D	RESEARCH & DEVELOPMENT
Pt	TOTAL PRESSURE	RDF	RADIO DIRECTION FINDER
PT(N)	PROCEDURE TURN	RDR	RADAR DEPARTURE ROUTE
PTO	PART TIME OPERATION		
PTT	PUSH TO TALK	REGS	REGULATIONS
PVASI	PULSATING VASI	REIL	RUNWAY END IDENTIFICATION LIGHTS
PWI	PROXIMITY WARNING INDICATOR		
		RG	RETRACTABLE GEAR
QDM	MAGNETIC BEARING TO FACILITY	RH	RELATIVE HUMIDITY
		RL	RUNWAY EDGE LIGHTS
QDR	MAGNETIC BEARING FROM FACILITY	RMI	RADIO MAGNETIC INDICATOR
QFE	ALTIMETER SETTING READS ZERO AT FIELD ELEVATION	RNAV	RANDOM AREA NAVIGATION
QK	QUICK FLASHING	RNP	REQUIRED NAVIGATION PERFORMANCE
QNE	ALTIMETER SETTING (29.92 HG / 1013.2 MB)		
		RO	REPORT OVER
QNH	ALTIMETER SETTING- LOCAL STATION PRESSURE	R/O	RECEIVE ONLY
		ROC	RATE OF CLIMB
		ROD	RATE OF DESCENT
R	RADIAL, RADAR, RECEIVE ONLY, RESTRICTED AREA	RPI	RUNWAY POINT OF INTERCEPTION
		RPM	REVOLUTIONS PER MINUTE
RAI	RUNWAY ALIGNMENT INDICATOR		
		R&R	REMOVE AND REPLACE
RAIL	RUNWAY ALIGNMENT INDICATOR LIGHTS	RRL	RUNWAY REMAINING LIGHTS
RAPCON	RADAR APPROACH CONTROL	RSC	RUNWAY SURFACE CONDITION
RAT	RAM AIR TURBINE	RSPT	REPORT STARTING PROCEDURE TURN
RB	RELATIVE BEARING, ROTATING BEACON	RT	RECEIVER/ TRANSMITTER
RBN	RADIO BEACON (MARINE)	RTO	REJECTED TAKEOFF

RTS	RETURN TO SERVICE	SL	SEA LEVEL
RV	RADAR VECTOR	SLP	SEA LEVEL PRESSURE
RVR	RUNWAY VISUAL RANGE	SM	STATUTE MILES
		SMOH	SINCE MAJOR OVERHAUL
RVSM	REDUCED VERTICAL SEPARATION MINIMUMS	S/N	SERIAL NUMBER
		SNAFU	SITUATION NORMAL-ALL FOULED UP
RWY TDZ	FIRST 3,000 FEET OF RUNWAY	SOB	SOULS ON BOARD
RX	RECEIVE, REPORT CROSSING	SODALS	SIMPLIFIED OMNIDIRECTIONAL APPROACH LIGHT SYSTEM
S	STANDARD, STRAIGHT-IN, SIMULTANEOUS, NDB HOMING SIGNAL	SOH	SINCE OVERHAUL
		SOV	SHUT-OFF VALVE
		SPB	SEA PLANE BASE
SAC	STRATEGIC AIR COMMAND	SPEC	SPECIFICATION
		SPOH	SINCE PROP OVERHAUL
SALS	SHORT APPROACH LIGHT SYSTEM	SPS	STALL PROTECTION SYSTEM
SALSF	SHORT APPROACH LIGHT SYSTEM W/SEQUENCED FLASHING LIGHTS	SQ	SQUAWK
		SRA	SPECIAL RULES AREA, SURVEILLANCE RADAR APPROACH
SAR	SEARCH AND RESCUE		
SAT	STATIC AIR TEMPERATURE	SSALF	SIMPLIFIED SHORT APPROACH LIGHT SYSTEM WITH SEQUENCED FLASHING LIGHTS
SB	SIDEBAND (HF COMM), SERVICE BULLETIN		
SCMOH	SINCE CHROME MAJOR OVERHAUL	SSALR	SIMPLIFIED SHORT APPROACH LIGHT SYSTEM WITH RAIL
SDF	SIMPLIFIED DIRECTIONAL FACILITY	SSALS	SIMPLIFIED SHORT APPROACH LIGHT SYSTEM
SEL	SINGLE-ENGINE LAND		
SFAR	SPECIAL FEDERAL AVIATION REGULATION	SSB	SINGLE SIDE BAND
		SST	SUPERSONIC TRANSPORT
SFL	SEQUENCED FLASHING LIGHTS	STAB	STABILIZER
		STAB AUG	STABILITY AUGMENTATION
SFRM	SINCE FACTORY REMANUFACTURE	STAR	STANDARD TERMINAL ARRIVAL ROUTE
SHS	SINCE HOT SECTION	STC	SUPPLEMENTAL TYPE CERTIFICATE
SIC	SECOND IN COMMAND		
SID	STANDARD INSTRUMENT DEPARTURE	STOH	SINCE TOP OVERHAUL
		STOL	SHORT TAKEOFF AND LANDING
SIGMET	SIGNIFICANT METEOROLOGICAL INFORMATION	SVFR	SPECIAL VFR

T	TAKEOFF MINIMUM, TONS, TRANSMIT		TPA	TRAFFIC PATTERN ALTITUDE
°T	TRUE (DEGREES)		T/R	THRUST REVERSER
TAC	TACAN, TERMINAL AREA CHART		TRACON	TERMINAL RADAR APPROACH CONTROL
TACAN	TACTICAL AIR NAVIGATION		TRSA	TERMINAL RADAR SERVICE AREA
TAS	TRUE AIR SPEED		T&S	TURN AND SLIP INDICATOR
TAT	TOTAL AIR TEMPERATURE		TSO	TECHNICAL STANDARD ORDER
TBO	TIME BETWEEN OVERHAULS		TT	TOTAL TIME
TC	TURN COORDINATOR, TRUE COURSE, TYPE CERTIFICATE		TTAE	TOTAL TIME AIRCRAFT & ENGINE
			TTSN	TOTAL TIME SINCE NEW
TCAS	TRAFFIC ALERT AND COLLISION AVOIDANCE SYSTEM		T-VASI	TEE VISUAL APPROACH SLOPE INDICATOR
			TVOR	TERMINAL VOR
TCH	THRESHOLD CROSSING HEIGHT		TW	TWEB ROUTE FORECAST
TCTA	TRANSCONTINENTAL CONTROL AREA		TWEB	TRANSCRIBED WEATHER BROADCAST
TDZ	TOUCHDOWN ZONE		TWR	CONTROL TOWER
TDZE	TOUCHDOWN ZONE ELEVATION		TX	TRANSMIT
TDZL	TOUCHDOWN ZONE LIGHTING		U	UNICOM, UNVERIFIED, UNTIL, UNIFORM, UP
TDZ/CL	TOUCHDOWN ZONE AND CENTERLINE LIGHTING		(U)	UNWATCHED
			UAG	UPPER ATMOSPHERE GEOPHYSICS
TEC	TOWER ENROUTE CONTROL		UCWA	URGENT CENTER WEATHER ADVISORY
TELEX	TELEPHONE EXCHANGE		UDF	UHF BAND DIRECTION FINDER
TERPS	TERMINAL INSTRUMENT APPROACH PROCEDURES		UFA	UNTIL FURTHER ADVISED
TET	TETRAHEDRON		UFN	UNTIL FURTHER NOTICE
TGL	TOUCH-AND-GO LANDING		UFO	UNIDENTIFIED FLYING OBJECT
TIT	TURBINE INLET TEMPERATURE		UHF	ULTRA-HIGH FREQUENCY
TLV	TRANSITION LEVEL		UIR	UPPER FLIGHT INFORMATION REGION
T/O	TAKE-OFF			
TOC	TAKE-OFF CONFIGURATION		UNICOM	UNIVERSAL COMMUNICATIONS
TODA	TAKE-OFF DISTANCE AVAILABLE		U/S	UNSERVICEABLE
TORA	TAKE-OFF RUN AVAILABLE			

USB	UPPER SIDEBAND	VOT	VOR TEST SIGNAL
USCG	US COAST GUARD	VOX	VOICE OPERATED
USCS	US CUSTOMS SERVICE	VFR	MILITARY TRAINING
USMC	US MARINE CORPS		ROUTE
USN	US NAVY	VRS	VOICE RESPONSE
USWB	US WEATHER BUREAU		SYSTEM
UTA	UPPER CONTROL AREA	VS	VERTICAL SPEED
UTC	COORDINATED	VSI	VERTICAL SPEED
	UNIVERSAL TIME		INDICATOR
		VSTL	VERTICAL SHORT
V	VISUAL DESCENT		TAKEOFF & LANDING
	POINT, VELOCITY,	VTOL	VERTICAL TAKEOFF
	VICTOR AIRWAY		AND LANDING
V2(L)(R)	2 BOX VASI	VVI	VERTICAL VELOCITY
	(LEFT OR RIGHT		INDICATOR
	SIDE OF RUNWAY)	V/V	VERTICAL VELOCITY
V4(L)(R)	4 BOX VASI		
	(LEFT OR RIGHT	W	WARNING AREA
	SIDE OF RUNWAY)	WAC	WORLD AERONAUTICAL
V12	12 BOX VASI (BOTH		CHART
	SIDES OF RUNWAY)	W/B	WEIGHT AND BALANCE
VASI	VISUAL APPROACH	WCA	WIND CORRECTION
	SLOPE INDICATOR		ANGLE
VDF	VHF BAND DIRECTION	WILCO	WILL COMPLY
	FINDER	WIP	WORK IN PROGRESS
VDP	VISUAL DESCENT	WOS	WEATHER OBSERVING
	POINT		STATION
VE	VISUAL EXEMPTED	WOW	WEIGHT ON WHEELS
VIB	VIBRATION	WS	WIND SPEED, WIND
VICE	INSTEAD/VERSUS		SHEAR, WEAK SIGNAL
VIP	VERY IMPORTANT	WSO	WEATHER SERVICE
	PERSON		OFFICE (NWS)
VFR	VISUAL FLIGHT RULES,	WX	WEATHER
VHF	VERY HIGH FREQUENCY	WXR	WEATHER RADAR
VLF	VERY LOW FREQUENCY		
VMC	VISUAL	X	CROSS, CLOSED
	METEOROLOGICAL	XCVR	TRANSCEIVER
	CONDITIONS	XMTR	TRANSMITTER
VNAV	VERTICAL	XPDR	TRANSPONDER
	NAVIGATION		
VOL	VOLUME	YD, Y/D	YAW DAMPER
VOLMET	METEOROLOGICAL		
	INFORMATION FOR	Z	ZULU (UTC),
	AIRCRAFT FLIGHT	ZULU	COORDINATED
VOR	VHF OMNI-		UNIVERSAL TIME
	DIRECTIONAL		
	RANGE STATION		
VORTAC	COLLOCATED VOR &		
	TACAN		

INDEX

A
abbreviations, 68
acronyms, 54
aerobatic flight, 32
aeronautical chart scales, 11
aircraft categories, 8
aircraft currency, 27
aircraft equipment suffixes, 15
aircraft lights, 31
aircraft loading, 8
AIRMET, 18
airport beacons, 29
airspeed holding, 38
airspeed limitations, 29
airworthiness, 27
alcohol, 27
alternate airports, 34
altitudes, IFR, 35
altitudes, minimum safe, 29
approach lighting systems, 39
ATC clearance void time, 34
ATC clearance items, 37
aviation calculations, 9

B
bank angle vs stall, 8

C
carbon monoxide, 48
checklists, 24
circle to land, 41
circling approach, 41
communication frequencies, 13
communications failure, 32, 36
communications IFR, 36
contact approach, 37
crosswind component chart, 5
cruise clearance, 37
cruising altitudes VFR, 31

D
dead reckoning, 2
decision height, 40
decompression sickness, 48
density altitude, 6
departures, IFR, 34

E
distance formula, 1
ditching, 51

emergency communications, 47
emergency locator transmitter (ELT), 50
emergency resuscitation, 48
engine failure, 47
Enroute Flight Advisory Service (EFAS), 20

F
final approach fix, 42
fire, 47
flight near other aircraft, 28
flight plan, 15
Frequency Spectrum, 63
fuel requirements, IFR, 34
fuel requirements, VFR, 29

G
glide slope, 38
ground to air signals, 52

H
hemispheric rule, 31
holding airspeed, 38
holding instructions, 37
hyperventilation, 48
hypoxia, 48

I
ice descriptions, 21
ice reporting criteria, 20
IFR recent experience, 34
initial approach fix, 41
inoperative instruments, 32
instruments required, 31, 35
intermediate approach segment, 42

L
light signals, 29
line of position, 4
localizer, 38

M
MACH vs TAS, 66

(82)

marker beacons, 38
mean aerodynamic chord, 8
medical conditions, 48
METAR/TAF, 16
metric measurements, 10
minimum descent altitude, 40
minimum safe altitudes, 29
missed approach, 41
Morse code, 14

N
NASA Reports, 33
Navaids, 13, 14
navigation formulas, 1, 9
NDB reception Range, 13
NOTAMs, 18
NTSB, reports to, 32, 33
numeric prefixes, 10

O
oxygen requirements, 31

P
parachutes, 32
phonetic alphabet, 14
pilot controlled lighting, 40
pilot currency, 27
pilot reports, 21
pilotage, 4
position reports, 35
preflight, 28
preventive maintenance, 33
procedure turns, 41

R
right of way, 28
rule of sixty, 3
running fix, 4
RVR, 40

S
safety belts, 28
scuba diving, 48
SIGMET, 18
signaling, 51, 52
solar still, 49
Standard Atmosphere, 65
standard weights, 7
survival at sea, 50

survival equipment, 49
survival kit, 49
survival on land, 48

T
time zones, 62
transponder codes, 15
transponder mode C, 32
turbulence reporting, 20
TWEB, 18

V
VFR weather minimums, 31
VFR-on-top, 37
visual approach, 37
VOR accuracy check, 34
VOR identification, 14
VOR reception altitudes, 14
VOR Test Frequencies, 64
VOT, 64
V-Speeds, 67

W
weather briefing format, 15
Weather Contractions, 22
Weight and Balance, 7
weight shift formula, 8
Wind Chill Factors, 53
winds aloft , 18